Play on Word

Devin Lonergan Holt

To : Jennifer

Have Fun & Godspeed !

—Devin Lonergan Holt

ISBN–13: 9781632694713
Library of Congress: 2018938160
Printed in the United States of America.
Cover design by Robin Black, Inspirio Design

Play on
Word

Contents

Seasonal Lessons

Post-Easter Lessons

Christmas Lessons

Final Lessons and Final Thoughts

To Anna, my greatest advocate and cheerleader,

To Sidney, my tenacious and wise advisor,

I love you both beyond words and am honored to have created
the lessons for you and with you. May we continue
to learn and grow in our faith together.

And, to every caregiver and child who play the lessons
together, have fun and Godspeed!

So...How do I do this?

Dear Reader,

It's easy. First, ask yourself, "why do I have this book?" If the answer is "a friend gave it to me," start with the New Testament lessons beginning with Week 10, called "Baby Jesus." It will be warm welcome to the book and a fun place to begin. If the answer is "my children have their faith foundations intact, but I want them to know more about the Bible," then begin with Week 1's "God's Creation" lesson. *Play on Word* can walk your family through the Bible lessons in order. *OR* If the answer is "I love Bible time with my children, but they just won't sit still long enough to hear the lesson!" then this book is definitely for you too. You can begin with any lesson, but Week 6, "The Walls of Jericho," might be a good one to show your children this book is different than any they have seen because they get to *PLAY* it.

After you select your lesson, review and consider the Note of Purpose for the chapter. It will help you focus and reflect on the lesson's main idea. And, although I've addressed these notes "Dear Parent," they're equally intended for grandparents, guardians, teachers, or anyone else in a position to nurture a child's faith.

Next, gather the toys or materials listed. You may find substitutions are necessary or desirable. The materials, for the most part, should be accessible in any household with young children. Then, as you read the Script with your child, remember the words in parentheses show your actions or movements. The words not in parentheses are the words you'll say aloud. You may even want to prop the book up so that your hands are free to play the lesson. In this way, your children will be able to hear your words, see the objects, touch the lesson, engage in their Bible time, and grow their faith.

Lastly, please know that children should never be left alone during *Play on Word* lessons. Some small toys or household items can be harmful to children in the absence of supervision. So *Play on Word* with caution and care. I organized the lessons with a weekly format in mind. You may choose to do more or less than one lesson per week.

May you enjoy the lessons and grow together in Christ!

Devin Lonergan Holt

Old Testament Lessons

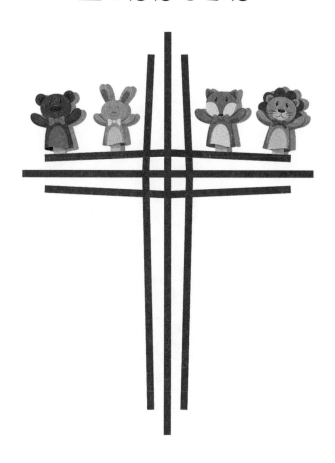

Week 1: God's Creation

BIBLE READING: Genesis 1 and 2:1–3

Dear Parent,

The goal of this week's lesson is to play with the story of Creation. Creation is the perfect place to start this faith journey with Bible playtime together. This lesson has more materials to collect than other lessons, but God created so very much on this earth for you and your child to enjoy. So have fun with the lesson. Let your children know where we came from. Let your children feel God's love by showing them everything God has created for us.

Materials:

Bible, small table lamp, large sheet of blue paper, medium-sized sheet of green paper, markers, flashlights, and figurines or toys in the form of a man and a woman

Script:

Do you know where we came from? Everything on the earth came from God. He started making and creating a very long time ago. Do you want to know how he did it?

(Let your child answer)

The Bible tells us the story. It says, "In the beginning God created the heavens and the earth" (Genesis 1:1). Everything was empty and dark. But God was there, over the waters. "Then God said, 'Let there be light'" (Genesis 1:3).

And there it was—light!

(Turn the table lamp on)

Then "God saw the light was good, and he separated the light from the darkness. God called the light 'day,' and the darkness he called 'night.' And there was evening, and there was morning—the first day" (Genesis 1:4–5).

And, that truly was the first full day in the whole world!

(Ask your child to turn the lamp off)

God is so amazing. He actually made day and night. Every day that passes in our own lives happens because God created that day for us. Do you want to know what God made on the second day? Let's find out.

(Ask your child to turn the lamp on)

Next, God said, "Let there be a vault," which means a big space, "between the waters to separate water from water." God called this big space the "sky."

(Lay out the blue paper)

It looks like we have our waters right here. And if we look out the window, we can see the sky God made too. That marks the end of the second day.

(Ask your child to turn the lamp off. Then ask your child to turn it back on, as you continue with the script)

14

Once again, "There was evening, and there was morning" (Genesis 1:8). The second day ended, and the third day began. God said, "Let the water under the sky be gathered to one place, and let dry ground appear" (Genesis 1:9).

> (Let your child put the green paper anywhere in the midst of the "water" [blue paper])

This green paper is our land, and "God called the dry ground 'land,' and the gathered waters he called 'seas.' And God saw that it was good" (Genesis 1:10). God wanted the land to have plants and trees, which will give the earth seeds and fruits. And again, God saw that it was good.

> (1. Draw flowers and trees together on the green paper. Make sure you leave enough space on the paper to draw in the rest of Creation over the course of the lesson)

> (2. Let your child turn the lamp off and turn it back on again as you say . . .)

Along came the evening, and then came the morning. The third day ended, and the fourth day began. After that, God said, "Let there be lights in the vault of the sky to separate the day from the night, and let them serve as signs to mark seasons and days and years" (Genesis 1:14). So God made the sun (our lamp), the moon, and the stars too.

> (1. Give your child the flashlights for the moon and stars. Enjoy the lights together)

> (2. Let your child turn the lamp off and turn it back on again)

Again, God saw it was good. Evening arrived, and then the next morning arrived. The fourth day ended, and the fifth day began. Now that the earth was created, God planned for life on earth. He wanted to make living creatures in the water and birds for the sky. So he created them. And once again, God saw that it was good.

> (1. Draw fish and birds together)

(2. Let your child turn the lamp off and turn it back on again)

There was another evening, and there was a new morning. The fifth day ended, and the sixth day began. God wanted the land to have living creatures too. He made livestock, wild animals, and all sorts of creatures, and God saw it was good too!

(Draw animals together)

God also said, "Let us make mankind in our image, in our likeness, so that they may rule over the fish in the sea and the birds in the air, over the livestock and all the wild animals, and over all the creatures that move along the ground" (Genesis 1:26). So he did. He made a man and a woman. "God saw all that he had made, and it was very good" (Genesis 1:31).

(1. Let your child put the toy man and woman on the land. Discuss together all they rule over)

(2. Let your child turn the lamp off. Do not have them turn it on yet)

There was evening, and that marked the end of the sixth day. At that point, the heavens and the earth were completed. By the seventh day, God finished his work. And God blessed the seventh day, and made it holy, because on it he rested from all the work of creating he had done.

(Let your child turn the lamp on)

Let's lay down and pretend to rest too.

My child, that is where you came from and where I came from. God worked so hard to make the earth and make it all good. Because God put us in charge to rule over the earth, it is our job to take care of it. So we must keep the earth and ourselves as good as we can.

God loves us so much. He gave us the world!

Week 2: Noah's Ark

BIBLE READING: Genesis 6:9 through 9:17

Dear Parent,

The goal of this week's lesson is to play with the story of Noah's Ark. For adults, Noah's Ark is a complicated story about the wicked state of the world and God's will to change it with a flood, which led to a new beginning. But it is also about obeying God's commands and trusting him to provide a future. The story might not have as much depth for children. For them, it might just be about building a big boat, bringing the animals two by two, and looking for rainbows.

Regardless, enjoy the story time today. Weave what you believe about this story into playtime with your children. Pass on your perspective and wisdom as you play together.

Materials:

Bible, toy tools, toy boat, people figurines, animal figurines, and a small twig

Script:

Today we're going to talk about a classic story in the Bible, *Noah's Ark*! A long time ago, the people on the earth were mean and grumpy. And I mean *everyone* was mean and grumpy . . . except Noah. God was not happy with how the world seemed to be more bad than good. So, God told Noah to build an ark, which is an enormous boat. Should we pretend to help Noah today? Let's do it!

(Play with the toys, and pretend to build the toy boat)

God told Noah how big to make the ark. It, of course, was much bigger than our toy boat. It was 300 by 50 by 30 cubits. That sounds pretty big, huh? It's about as big as two football fields! God also told Noah the boat needed a roof, a lower deck, a middle deck, and an upper deck. God told Noah that he was going to bring a flood to destroy everything on the earth except Noah, his wife, his kids, their wives, and two of every living creature. God told Noah to bring enough food for everyone too! Whew! That's a lot of work to get done in the seven days God gave Noah to prepare!

Can we help Noah get everything and everyone on the boat? What kinds of animals did Noah bring to the ark? What kinds of foods did he pack for all of them to eat? Did the gorillas eat the same foods as the giraffes?

(As you continue the lesson, play with the boat and the animals)

It is so awesome that God spoke to Noah. And, it is so awesome that Noah obeyed God . . . because the rain soon started, and the waters rose. It rained for forty days and forty nights, until the whole world was completely filled with water. Even after the rain stopped, the water covered the earth for one hundred and fifty days!

Do you think Noah ever got scared? Through the ark's window, all that water probably looked scary, dark, and powerful! I don't believe Noah got scared. He already trusted God enough to build the ark and go inside. Noah probably felt safe and calm. We all need to trust God when we are doing his work. During those times, in particular, God is watching out for us and helping us.

At some point, Noah knew it would soon be time to get off the boat. He sent out a dove to see if enough of the water had dried up. It took a few tries, but eventually the dove returned with an olive branch in its beak.

(Show your child the twig, and continue with the script)

The olive branch was a sign that more ground had been uncovered and plants had even started growing again. Once the earth was totally dry, God told Noah to come out of the ark. God blessed Noah and said, "Be fruitful and increase in number and fill the earth" (Genesis 9:1). In addition, God instructed Noah and his family to be good and never hurt each other.

God also promised he would never flood the earth again. God made the rainbow as a sign of this promise. Let's help everyone get off the boat.

(Play with toy animals)

When we remember Noah's ark, we can think about more than just the animals going in two by two. We can think about:

* ✳ how important it is to be good to every person and animal in the world. We don't want the world to be a wicked place again, like it was a long time ago.

* ✳ trusting God during stormy days and sunny days. God will stop the rain. He'll provide a place for us to live and grow. He always keeps his promises . . . just like the rainbow reminds us.

Week 3: The Call of Abram

BIBLE READING: Genesis 12:1–9

Dear Parent,

    The goal of this week's lesson is to teach your child how to listen for God and follow his directions. If God tells us to do something, then we must do it. God called Abram to leave the land he had always known. God promised his blessings to Abram, and Abram promised obedience.

Materials:

Bible, one small toy, and a deck of cards

Script:

    I know that you know it is really important to do what I say. If I say, "Pick up this toy," then, as my child, you should pick up this toy as quickly as you possibly can. Right?

(Put one toy on the floor)

Please pick this toy up.

(Wait for your child pick it up)

Very good! I said pick up the toy, and you did! But what if the job I give you seems really hard? You still have to obey me, right? Now, pick these up!

(Throw a loose deck of cards up in the air and let them all fall to the ground. Laugh together. As you continue with the lesson, pick them up together)

If my instructions sometime seem difficult, you still have to follow through with them because I love you, because I know what is best for you, and, simply, because I said so. Right?

Well, the same can be said for God's instructions. Actually, God's instructions are even more important than my instructions because God is more powerful and more knowledgeable than me! He is the most wonderful and important thing in the whole world! And, like a parent, he loves us and knows what is best for us.

A long time ago, there was a man named Abram. God told him to leave the place he had always lived and go to a new place, which God would lead him to. God told Abram:

> Go from your country, your people and your father's
> household to the land I will show you. I will make
> you into a great nation and I will bless you; I will
> make your name great, and you will be a blessing. . . .
> and all peoples on earth will be blessed through you.
> (Genesis 12:1–3)

Do you want to know what Abram did? He obeyed! Abram did exactly what God told him to do. He gathered up his family and everything he owned. Then he went to the place where God told him to go. What God asked Abram to do was *hard*. But Abram still obeyed.

When God asks you to do something, you must do it too. If you feel God in your heart telling you to be nice or to do something good, then you must obey as quickly as possible, because God loves you. God knows what is best for you. And more simply, you must do it because God said so. No matter how big *(point to the deck of cards)* or how small *(point to the one toy)* the job is, we must obey God and always do what he says.

Week 4:
Moses Parts the Red Sea

BIBLE READING: Exodus 14

Dear Parent,

    The goal of this week's lesson is to teach your children that the Lord will come to the rescue. If there is danger, God can fight for his people. God can keep us safe. God can save our lives. He saves our lives every day.

Materials Needed:

Bible, 13 x 9 baking pan, 2 cups of water, and a small towel

Script:

    Have you ever heard the word *slave*? A slave is someone who doesn't get to do what they want to do. It's a person who is forced to work for someone else without getting paid for it. A long time ago, the people who believed in God were slaves for the king of Egypt. The king was called the pharaoh. He was not nice to the slaves, and he "made their lives bitter with harsh labor in brick and mortar and with all kinds of work in the fields; in all their harsh labor the Egyptians used them ruthlessly" (Exodus 1:14) without caring for them.

The people of God were tired and sore, but they had to keep on working under those conditions for years and years. Through that time, God's people always felt scared of what might happen to them under the pharaoh's rule.

Can you imagine how that might have felt? We are God's people. What if we were alive during that time so long ago? Can you imagine you and me, working in the scorching heat to build buildings and work in the fields without getting paid any money? Can you imagine if you dropped a brick on your foot and felt like you couldn't work anymore? The pharaoh's guards would force you to stand up and work even faster than before your injury. That sounds scary, doesn't it?

Well, that is how God's people were forced to live until a man named Moses came along. God told Moses to ask Pharaoh to let God's people go. It took a lot of convincing, but, finally, Pharaoh agreed to free God's people. So God's people left as quickly as they could. They went through the wilderness toward the Red Sea. Let's pour our water into this pan. This will be our "Red Sea."

(Pour the two cups of water into the pan)

One night, as God's people camped by the sea, they woke up and saw Pharaoh's armies coming after them. Oh no, Pharaoh had changed his mind! He was coming to capture them and enslave them again! God's people were so scared! They did not want to go back to Egypt. But they had nowhere else to go. The Red Sea was in front of them, and Pharaoh's armies were behind them!

Moses said to the people, "Do not be afraid. Stand firm and you will see the deliverance the LORD will bring you today . . . . The LORD will fight for you; you need only to be still" (Exodus 14:13–14). And Moses was right. The Lord told Moses to lift up his staff, stretch out his hand over the sea, and divide it. Can you believe it actually happened? The people were able to cross through the walls of water on dry ground and have a clear path to a new land.

Isn't that amazing? Parting the waters and making a path through the middle of the sea for God's people to walk through was a miracle! Moses created this path for the people. The path led to safety and freedom. They would not have to go back to being slaves for Pharaoh.

Let's look at our pan of water. Let's see if we can part these waters. First, we can try Moses' way, and stretch out our hands over the water to divide it.

(Spread your arms apart)

Hmmm. This doesn't seem to be working. Well, let's put our hands in the water and try that way.

(Using your hands, try to separate the water and keep it spread apart enough for passage)

That didn't work either. Maybe we could try to shake the pan. Gosh, if we can't even part the waters in this pan, how could Moses part an entire sea of water? One difference is that Moses had God's help. With God, Moses had all the power and strength he needed to part the waters.

God fought for his people. God made them safe. God saved their lives.

So if something scares us, we can always remember what Moses said. "Do not be afraid. Stand firm and you will see the deliverance the Lord will bring you today . . . . The Lord will fight for you; you need only to be still."

And believe that God will fight for you. God will make you safe. God saves our lives. God saves us every day.

Week 5:
The Ten Commandments

BIBLE READING: Deuteronomy 4:13; Exodus 20:1–17

Dear Parent,

The goal of this week's lesson is to teach your children that God provides rules for how we are to live. Are we perfect in them? No, that is where Jesus saves us. However, as we raise our children, it's important for them to know that the rules we give to them ultimately come from the rules God gave us. Let us teach them the rules and encourage them to strive for obedience.

Materials Needed:

Bible, notebook paper, pencil, and markers

Script:

Today we are going to talk about rules. Can you think of any rules we have around our home?

(Let your child answer)

Yes! That is definitely a rule we have around here. Do you know why we have rules?

(Let your child answer)

We have rules to keep you safe and to help you know how to make good choices. Do you know where rules come from?

(Let your child answer)

That was a hard question. Most rules come from God. He put them in the Bible. So if we ever need to see them or need help remembering them, they are easy to find!

There are ten rules or commandments for us to follow. And yes, even though I am the one who enforces your rules, I must follow these ten rules too! Let's write the numbers one through ten on this piece of paper. We can put "Number 1" on the top line and then write the rest of the numbers, all the way down to "Number 10."

(Help your child write the numbers)

Very Good! Can you believe that almost all of the rules we need to follow fit into those ten spaces? Actually, there are a few more very important rules that God told us about through Jesus, but we'll get to those another week. Let's look at the Bible together. The rules are listed in the book of Exodus, in chapter 20, verses 1 through 17. They can be hard for kids to understand, but we can talk about them together!

And let's decorate the numbers as we discuss each rule. We can make them as beautiful as possible because we are thankful for these rules.

Number 1: I am your God.

This one is great. It is a reminder of who is in charge: God.

Number 2: Only worship me (God).

Well, that's easy for us! Of course, we don't worship anyone other than God!

Number 3: Don't misuse my name (God's name).

Have you ever heard anyone do that? For example, if someone is surprised, they say, "Oh, my You-know-who" instead of saying "Oh, wow!" or "Oh, gosh." This rule is important because God only wants his name to be used in prayer, worship, sharing, and learning.

Number 4: Keep Sabbath or Sunday special.

It is hard to slow things down on our day off from work or school, but God really wants us to take one day of the week for rest, worship, and thinking about him. Some people, like doctors and police officers, might still have to work on Sunday, so their families can take a Sabbath on a different day of the week, such as Wednesday.

Number 5: Honor your mother and father.

I love this one! God wants you to listen and obey *me*. And I also need to listen and obey my parents (your grandparents).

Number 6: Don't hurt other people.

God wants us all to get along and live in a peaceful world together.

Number 7: Once you get married, stay with your husband or wife.

This one doesn't apply to you quite yet, but it is never too early to start praying for a happy and healthy marriage.

Number 8: Don't steal.

Never take anything that isn't yours. You can work hard to earn a lot of things, but you should never take something that doesn't belong to you.

Number 9: Don't lie.

We have to tell the truth all the time. Even if it is bad news or if it means confessing something we did wrong, God doesn't want us to ever lie to him or each other.

Number 10: Don't take things from your friends and neighbors.

This one helps you to be a good friend and neighbor!

Wow! All the rules in the world come down to these ten. Do you think we can be perfect all the time in all of these rules?

(Let your child answer)

No. We can't. And God isn't super angry with us when we do break them. Do you know why? Because of Jesus! God learned we couldn't follow all of these rules perfectly. We are human. We make mistakes. And so God sent Jesus to earth. Jesus is someone who could be, and actually was, perfect. In his whole life, Jesus never broke one of these rules. Can you imagine? He never had a time out, he never had a treat taken away, and he never got in trouble. He was truly perfect. We are so lucky because Jesus gave his perfection to us as a gift. So when God sees us, he doesn't see the things we did wrong. When God sees us, he sees Jesus' perfection, the good in our hearts, and the strong way we love Jesus.

Ultimately, are the rules important? Yes! Should we try our best every day? Yes! Will God forgive us and love us no matter what . . . thanks to Jesus? Yes! I thank God for these rules though. They are great guidelines for the kind of person I want to be. How about you?

Week 6:
The Walls of Jericho

BIBLE READING: Joshua 5:13–6:20

Dear Parent,

The goal of this week's lesson is to talk about God's promises. The world can be a hard place to live. Some people are dishonest. Some people don't follow through with their commitments. But there is someone in this world who will never let us down: God. God is always honest. God will always come through. God will always keep his promises. Even on our hardest days, God is there to help us "break down walls" and achieve glory in his name.

Materials:

Bible, blankets, dining room or playroom furniture, two sleeping bags, and a toy trumpet or musical instrument

Script:

Look at our materials for today's lesson! We are going to be busy today! Let's build a fort!

> *(Move the chairs into a circle with the backs of the chairs toward the inside of the circle. Make sure the circle is big enough for you and your child to sit inside, yet small enough for the blankets to drape over the tops of the chair backs to provide a "ceiling." Drape the remaining blankets over the rest of the chairs to provide the look of "walls")*

We did it! And, this is not just any fort. We're pretending this is our own little city of Jericho. Jericho was a city that was strongly built a very long time ago. Jericho was completely surrounded by walls. We need to pretend that our blanketed walls are enormously tall walls made of brick and stone. Can we do that?

Right now, we are outside the city, but back then the people lived inside the city and inside the walls. Shall we go in?

> *(Crawl inside together)*

Inside the city of Jericho, there weren't any churches. There weren't even any people who believed in God. In fact, God wasn't happy with the city of Jericho at all. So God sent down an angel, and not just any angel. This angel was the commander of all the angels in the army of God.

The angel commander sent a message to a real army commander named Joshua. Between the angel talking to Joshua and God talking to Joshua, Joshua got his next assignment. Joshua was supposed to lead his army to fight battles for God and fulfill God's plans. That is a pretty big job, right?

Well, Joshua bowed down to the angel and was ready for God's exact instructions. God wanted Joshua to walk his army of men around the entire city of Jericho once a day, for six days. Then, on the seventh day, Joshua was supposed to walk the army around the city seven times in a row. After that, the priests were supposed to sound the trumpets, and Joshua, along with his army, was supposed to shout out in the name of the Lord.

34

God promised that, if Joshua did all this, the walls of the city would fall down. He also promised that the armies could then get into the city and take over. Let's think about that. God made a promise to Joshua, and he broke down the walls for Joshua to achieve God's glory and plan.

Joshua did not hesitate or wonder what to do next. He just followed God's instructions. He believed in God's promise. Let's follow the instructions too. Let's march around the city once.

(Walk in a circle around the blanket fort)

Now we should lay in our sleeping bag and wait for Day number 2. Goodnight!

(Lay down, wait a few seconds, and proceed with the script)

Good morning! It is Day 2. Let's march around the city once.

(Repeat above steps accordingly as you act out Day 3–6)

Now we should lay in our sleeping bag and wait for Day number 3. Goodnight!

Good morning! It is Day 3. Let's march around the city once.

Now we should lay in our sleeping bag and wait for Day number 4. Goodnight!

Good morning! It is Day 4. Let's march around the city once.

Now we should lay in our sleeping bag and wait for Day number 5. Goodnight!

Good morning! It is Day 5. Let's march around the city once.

Now we should lay in our sleeping bag and wait for Day number 6. Goodnight!

Good morning! It is Day 6. Let's march around the city once.

Now, we should lay in our sleeping bag and wait for Day number 7. Goodnight! Day 7 is going to be exciting! It's the big day when the Lord promised to break down the walls!

Good morning! Time to wake up! It is Day 7. Let's march around the city seven times!

(Walk in a circle around the blanket fort 7 times)

Oh, my! I am almost dizzy from all this walking! Now the trumpets will sound!

(Sound the toy instrument)

Now we will yell, "We love God and believe in his promises!"

(Yell together)

Now the wall will be broken down!

(Make the blanketed wall fall down for your child. If you can do it without him or her noticing how it falls, it will be even more effective for the message)

Wow! These walls collapsed, just like the walls around the city of Jericho so long ago. How amazing! God's promise was real! He broke down the walls to fight battles for good and fulfill his plans! It took a lot of instruction-following on Joshua's part and on our part today as we played the lesson—but it worked! God did what he promised to do! We can always be sure God will keep his promises and that he can help us "break down the walls" of any problem in our lives.

Week 7: David and Goliath

BIBLE READING: 1 Samuel 17

Dear Parent,

The goal of this week's lesson is to show your children that, regardless of the size of the next challenge, they can prevail with faith in God.

MATERIALS:

Bible, tape measure, five wadded-up sheets of paper, a large rubber band, and a tree, doorway, or structure that is over nine feet tall

Script:

Have you ever heard of the Bible story about David and Goliath? It is such a great story about believing in God and how believing in God can help you solve problems. I want to tell you more about that story today. But first, what are some problems we have in our lives right now?

(Let your child answer. Everyone's life is different. You might be struggling with an ill grandparent, a death in the family, a bully, etc. Take time to identify and talk about this problem together)

Well, David came across a problem too . . . a big one. A war was raging between his people, the people of Israel, and the Philistines. The biggest, strongest, tallest, and fiercest Philistine warrior came forward to challenge any of David's people who were willing to fight him. This Philistine warrior had a big-sounding name too: Goliath. He truly was a giant.

Let's figure out how big this giant really was. I am only *(measure how tall you are)* feet tall, and you are only *(measure how tall your child is)* feet tall. The Bible says Goliath was "over nine feet tall!" (1 Samuel 17:4 NLT). Let's see how big that is.

(Unroll the tape measure to nine feet)

Wow! That is huge! Let's see if we can find something around our home that big.

(Walk around together to identify something about nine feet tall)

That is as big as this *(insert the name of your nine-foot-tall structure)*! Can you imagine going up against something or someone that big? Goliath's plan was to fight one person from Israel. And if Goliath won, everyone in Israel would become servants to the Philistines. But if someone from Israel won, the Philistines would become the servants.

Goliath didn't think any one person could beat him. He thought his plan would win the war. So every day, Goliath came forward at the battlefield and waited for someone to step up and fight. As you can imagine, no one from Israel wanted to fight someone that big. Not only was his size a scary and intimidating problem, but people were also afraid to fight because of how Goliath looked: "He wore a bronze helmet, and his coat of mail weighed 125 pounds. He also wore bronze leg armor, and he carried a bronze javelin on his shoulder" (1 Samuel 17:5–6 NLT). With his spears and javelins, which are like swords you can throw, he looked unstoppable and unbeatable.

Forty days passed, and no one came forward to fight. No one could solve this big problem. Until one day, a young boy named David was checking on his older brothers who were by the battlefield. David was the youngest of eight brothers. From where he stood, he saw Goliath. And he heard Goliath's challenge.

David said, "Let no man's heart fail because of himself. I will go and fight." Everyone warned David he was too young and too small to fight. They also told David he shouldn't fight because Goliath was a man used to fighting wars. But David felt confident. He had been protecting sheep in his flock. He knew God didn't save him from lions and bears just to have him get hurt by this giant.

David also said that Goliath would never win because Goliath was fighting against people who believed in the living God. David trusted that since God was with him, he could win against anything . . . even Goliath.

People tried to put armor on David to help protect him, but David took it back off. He didn't want it. He had God as his protecting armor. David chose five stones from the stream and got his sling, which is how he planned to send the rocks up nine feet in the air to reach Goliath.

Let's make some stones out of paper. Let's tear them in half, wad them up real tight, and throw them up nine feet high. Maybe we can even use this rubber band to make the "stones" go up higher.

(Go through the motions of throwing the rocks. Play together as you try to get the "stones" to the top of the nine-foot structure)

Doesn't nine feet seem too tall for us to fight and win with these five rocks? Don't we seem too small to succeed? Well, nothing is impossible when you believe in God and have faith in God.

Do you want to know how the story ended? When Goliath saw David, he said out loud that he would easily win. When David heard Goliath, he said, "You come against me with sword and spear and javelin, but I come against you in the name of the LORD Almighty, the God of the armies of Israel, whom you have defied. This day the LORD will deliver you into my hands, and I'll strike you down" (1 Samuel 17:45–46).

David continued on and told Goliath that, after his victory, all the earth would know how awesome God is. Then the Philistine came closer to the battle line, and David went in even closer. David reached for one of his smooth rocks, put it in the sling, and sent it up; it hit Goliath right on the forehead. Goliath fell forward, flat onto the ground. David had won.

What an amazing story! David believed in God and his protection, and he came out standing. David was okay. And everyone knew how awesome God is.

Obviously, we can't go throwing rocks, even fake rocks, at everything that scares us. Sometimes our way to win might be to report a problem to an adult, visit someone in the hospital, or simply get down on our knees to pray to God for help and for strength. If we do that, we will be like David. We will come out standing. We will be okay. And everyone will know how awesome God is.

Week 8: Solomon's Temple

BIBLE READING: 1 Kings 6

Dear Parent,

The goal of this week's lesson is to teach your child about doing God's work. As you know, we can't do anything to *earn* God's love. God gracefully bestows it upon us. However, when we look around, there is work to do. People need to be fed. Prayers need to be said. Churches need to be built. And the Word needs to be spread. Yes, we have a lot of work to do. But we do this work with bright eyes and full hearts. We do it to glorify God.

King Solomon worked with this kind of vigor in the Old Testament days. He built a magnificent house for the Lord. Interestingly enough, after eleven years of building and perfecting the temple, God loved him no more and no less. So then, was the work for nothing? Definitely not! Solomon tirelessly and generously built a house for his Lord! What devotion and glory he gave to God! May we all do God's work with the same joy, vibrancy, and intensity as Solomon.

Materials:

Bible, blocks, small sticks, and costume jewelry

Script:

I have a story about working for God I want to share with you.

(Open the Bible to 1 Kings, chapter 6)

All of the words in this whole chapter talk about one job planned by one man. The man's name was Solomon. Solomon decided to build a house for God. That was a great idea, right?

Let's learn about Solomon and the house he built for God, while we build a house for God using our blocks!

(Begin building together)

If I was going to build a house for God, I would want it to be amazing, wouldn't you? Well, Solomon was determined the house he built for God would be *amazing* too. So he worked on this house for eleven years! That's longer than you have even been alive! Solomon worked and worked. Solomon knew exactly the length he wanted to build it. He knew exactly how wide he wanted to build it.

(Continue to build together as you follow the script)

He made a patio with a roof attached on the outside of the house. He made an inner sanctuary, or worship room, on the inside of the house. He added other rooms, which he called side chambers, all around the house. He planted flowers and trees to make beautiful gardens for the house too. Doesn't it sound wonderful?

Now, why do you think Solomon built this house for the Lord? He didn't do it to make God love him more. God loves everyone just the same. He didn't do it so that he would end up in heaven. Solomon simply wanted to work for God.

Have you ever seen me work for God?

(Let your child answer. If needed, help your child with the answer based on the work you have done—teaching Sunday school, preparing food for a sick friend, praying for others, etc.)

You bet I have! It doesn't matter how big or small the task may have seemed at the time, I was working for God. Why do you think I did that? I didn't do it so God would love me more; God loves everyone just the same. I didn't do it so I would end up in heaven one day; God gave us Jesus so that everyone can go to heaven just the same. I did it because I, like Solomon, simply wanted to work for God.

Let's start decorating our little house for God, while I tell you about how Solomon kept on working, giving, and loving the Lord with his efforts.

(Lay out the rest of your materials)

Solomon knew which parts of the house he wanted to be made of cypress wood and which parts he wanted to be made of olive wood. We can put our sticks of wood in different places just like Solomon. Solomon added gold anywhere and everywhere he could! We can arrange our jewelry around our house to make it sparkle like Solomon made the Lord's house sparkle. Gosh, Solomon worked out every detail, didn't he?

It must have been magnificent. After eleven years of hard work, I imagine that house for God was the most beautiful thing anyone had ever seen. All that work, and God loved him just the same. When we do our work for God around our home and community, I hope we can have as much energy, as many ideas, and as much heart as our Dear Solomon.

Week 9: God's Plans

BIBLE READING: Jeremiah 29:11–13

Dear Parent,

The goal of this week's lesson is to understand God's plans for each of us. God knows what we did yesterday, what we are doing today, and what we will do tomorrow. Each of us is just one out of seven billion people in the entire world, yet God's plans for us are individualized and specific. As you go about your daily work, keep in mind God prepared your day today.

Materials:

Bible, one calendar from a past year, one calendar from this year, and one calendar for next year (optional)

Script:

Did you know God has a plan for you? He knows how he wants you to grow all year long. He knows where you have been. He knows where you are. He knows where you are going to be. The Bible talks about God's plans for you. It says, "'For I know the plans I have for you, declares the LORD, 'plans to prosper you and not to harm you, plans to give you hope and a future'" (Jeremiah 29:11–13).

Doesn't that make you feel good? It makes me feel ready for anything today. Speaking of plans, do you know what a calendar is?

(Let your child answer)

It is a big chart that shows the days in this whole year. Let's look and see. Here is today on the calendar. God has known for a long time that we would sit here together on this day of *(insert today's date)*. He knew you would grow closer to him today because of the time we're spending together learning about him and worshipping him while we play . . . today. God had this plan for you and me!

Now, what day is your birthday?

(Let your child answer)

Let's find it on the calendar. Here it is!

(Depending on whether or not your child's birthday has already happened in this calendar-year, follow the corresponding portion of the script below as you point out the date on this year's calendar)

Birthday Already Passed:

Do you remember what we did on your birthday?

(Let child answer)

Yes, we did *(insert birthday details here)*. God knew we were going to do that on your birthday. He knew where we'd be and who we'd be with! He knew we would celebrate the blessing that you are. He knew we would start another year of growing closer to him. He knew how much you had grown since last year's birthday. He knows how much you will grow before next year. Isn't that wonderful? God has a plan for you!

Birthday Yet to Come:

Do you know what our plans are for your birthday?

(Let child answer)

Well, God knows! He already knows where we'll be! He knows who we will be with! He knows that we will celebrate the blessing that you are. He knows that you will start another year of growing closer to him. He knows where you will have come from this year, where he wants you to go, and how much you will grow. He knows the plans for you that we don't even know. Isn't that wonderful? God has a plan for you!

Next, let's look at Christmas. Do you know when Christmas is? It is December the twenty-fifth!

(Point out December 25 on the calendar)

That will be a wonderful day, a day in which we will celebrate Jesus' birth! Do you know where we will be? Will we be at our house this year, or will we be at *(insert the name of a relative's or friend's house that you have been to for a holiday)*? Will there be a gift? Will there be any decorations? How will we honor and worship Jesus that day? Even if we haven't set our plans yet, God knows where we will be on Christmas. God has a plan for you and for me.

Let's look at how many days are in this calendar. Wow, there are so many days. There are 365 days in here. And God knows where you will be on every single one of them. God has a plan for you!

(Enjoy this time to talk about your child's year, your experiences this year as a parent, and those of relatives or friends. Using the calendars, elaborate on some dates of this year that have already passed [Examples: your child's best friend's birthday party, a significant day for you at work, the first day of school]. Elaborate on some future dates when you have planned events, trips, or celebrations. You can also reminisce about good dates when you celebrated with God.

47

You can mention sad dates or, perhaps, a day when you or someone you know struggled. Let your child know that God was there on those days too)

Our wonderful, loving, and huge God has a plan for each person in the world. That is seven billion people! How does he keep them all straight? I don't know how, but he does. Maybe he has seven billion calendars? Either way, he is amazing. He is the one and only God, and I love him.

NEW TESTAMENT LESSONS

Week 10: Baby Jesus

BIBLE READING: Luke 2:6–7

Dear Parent,

   The goal of this week's lesson is to talk about Jesus—the man who saved the world, the King of kings, the Prince of Peace, our Savior, the Messiah, and so much more. Yes, Jesus is many things, and yet he started out as an infant just like the rest of us. Today, show your children the human side of Jesus. Let your children relate to him. Let them feel close to him and identify with him.

Materials:

Your baby pictures, your child's baby pictures, and a baby doll

Script:

Let's talk about babies. Do we know anyone who is a baby right now, or anyone who has a baby right now?

(Let your child answer)

Do you know who used to be a baby?

(Let your child answer)

You did! Here are some baby pictures of you. You were so cute.

(Tell your child a cute or funny story from when he or she was a baby. Look through the pictures)

Do you know who else used to be a baby?

(Let your child answer)

I did! My parents told me I used to *(insert a cute or funny story about you from your infancy or childhood)*, when I was a baby.

(Look through your baby pictures)

Do you know who else used to be a baby?

Jesus did! Sometimes when I think about Jesus, I think of a king or the greatest man in the whole wide world, and those two things are true. But it is also important to think about where Jesus came from and how he started his life.

You have heard the Christmas story many times, but let's talk about it today. Baby Jesus was born in a stable instead of a hospital. He laid in a manger instead of a crib. But, otherwise, Jesus started out as a tiny baby just like you did.

Sometimes it helps me feel closer to Jesus when I think about how he began his life, the same size as I was when I started mine. Look at this baby doll.

(Pick up the baby doll)

It's about the same size as a real baby. So Jesus looked like this when he was born. When he was a baby, he had the same two eyes to see the big world from his tiny bed—similar to yours and mine. He had the same nose to smell his mother's milk and maybe some not-so-clean animals in the stable—similar to yours and mine.

As a baby, he had two ears to hear his mom, Mary, and his earthly dad, Joseph, say "I love you, and I am glad you are here"—similar to your ears and mine. He had a mouth to cry out of when he needed something—similar to yours and mine.

Now you are *(insert your child's age)* years old. Well, Jesus was *(insert the same age)* years old at one time too. When you go outside, you see the sky and the sun, right?

(Take the baby doll outside to see the sky and sun)

Jesus went outside when he wanted to see the sky and sun too! When you are sad, your heart hurts, right?

(Hold, cuddle, and comfort the baby doll)

When Jesus was sad, his heart hurt too! You like to play every day, right?

(Play with the baby doll)

Jesus liked to play every day too! You eat a few times a day, right?

(Pretend to feed the baby doll)

Jesus ate a few times a day too!

Jesus was like you. You are like him. So he understands how you feel, and this will never change. When you are ten years old, you'll need to remember that Jesus was once ten years old. When you are fifteen years old, you'll need to remember that Jesus was once fifteen. So you can be close to Jesus at any age. And you can always rely on Jesus to know how you are feeling. You can talk to Jesus about anything when you pray, and he will understand . . . because he has probably been through something similar.

Jesus is and will always be the King of kings. Jesus is the Prince of Peace. Jesus is called the greatest man in the world because he saved our lives and brought us closer to God. But through your worship and praise of him, don't forget to feel close to Jesus too. Jesus started out just like you and me—so that one day he could save the lives of you and me.

Week 11:
Boy Jesus at the Temple

BIBLE READING: Luke 2:43–52

Dear Parent,

The goal of this week's lesson is, as always, to help your children feel ever closer to Jesus. As we established last week, Jesus was once a kid too. He has more in common with your children than they realize. These commonalities can give insight, demonstrate Jesus' empathy, and truly bring your children closer to his heart.

So was Jesus indeed once a kid? Yes. Was he remarkable and perfect even in his youth? Yes. Did he start teaching others about God's love at a young age? Amazingly, yes. What an inspiring lesson for all of us. We are never too young to teach others about God's love.

Materials:

Bible, coats, blanket, and a small bag, tote, or suitcase

Script:

Can you think of a time we went on a trip or had a family reunion?

(Let your child answer. Listen to the answer and discuss the trip. Even if it was a trip across town to visit a friend or relative, it will help your child grasp today's lesson)

Yes! We did take that trip! Do you know who else used to take trips? Jesus did!

His family went to Jerusalem every year for the Feast of the Passover. It was a big family tradition. His relatives and friends went too. Doesn't that sound like fun? I am imagining Jesus at age twelve, and I feel sure he was so excited. Let's pretend like we are traveling to Jerusalem with Jesus too. We will celebrate Passover in Jerusalem with Jesus, Mary, Joseph, relatives, and friends.

First, we should get packed! What should we bring?

(Let your child answer)

Great! Let's put that in our bag! What else should we pack in our bags? We will need our coats. Should we take our favorite blanket? What else should we bring?

(Let your child answer. Pack the rest of the items together)

What do you think Jesus packed back when he traveled? I think he probably packed a cloak or coat too. There is a good chance he may have had a favorite blanket. You and Jesus have so much in common, which means you are so much the same!

When they were traveling to Jerusalem, who do you think Jesus wanted to travel next to? He would definitely have wanted to sit with you, if you were there! Who else could he have traveled next to? He could position himself next to his mom. Could a cousin or neighborhood friend have been beside him too? Maybe so!

It is so fun to think of boy Jesus in this context. Last week, we talked about Jesus starting his life as a baby, just like you. And this week, we're talking about Jesus being a kid, just like you. Even though we are living two thousand years later, there are some things that don't change over the years. There are some things we can understand about Jesus as a kid because I used to be a kid . . . and you still are a kid!

Are you curious to know what happened on Jesus' trip? There is a story in the Bible about a particular family trip when Jesus was twelve. It's right here in the Gospel of Luke.

(Open the Bible)

Well, after the feast and party were over, everyone started to go home, except Jesus. He stayed behind. There were so many people on the trip in Mary and Joseph's group, they didn't realize Jesus wasn't with them on the way home!

Are you curious about what Jesus did in Jerusalem without Mary and Joseph?

He stayed at the temple, which was like being at church. He sat with the teachers, talking with them about God. All who heard him were amazed at his understanding of God and his answers to the questions being asked. He was so young, and yet, so wise.

Eventually, Mary and Joseph realized Jesus wasn't with them on the trek home, and they hurried back to Jerusalem. Upon their arrival, they found Jesus in the temple. Mary explained how worried she had been. But Jesus calmly said to his mom, "Didn't you know I had to be in my Father's house?" (Luke 2:49).

At twelve years old, Jesus was already doing God's work. He was spreading God's love, and teaching people how to love their neighbor. This doesn't mean I will ever let you out of my sight on a trip! But it does mean that, just like Jesus, you are not too young to help teach other people about God's love.

Week 12: Jesus' Baptism

BIBLE READING: Matthew 3:13–17

Dear Parent,

    The goal of this week's lesson is to help your children understand baptisms. Baptisms are such cleansing gifts from God. In preparation for the lesson, take time to remember baptisms that you have seen. As you share Jesus' baptism story today, help your children feel cleansed. Help your children feel humbled and closer to God. May you both feel humbled and closer to God.

MATERIALS:

    Bible, baptism photos, and a bucket of water or bath tub

Script:

    Do you know what a baptism is?

(Let your child answer)

It is a special ritual and process that someone goes through when they enter God's family and become a *Christian*, which is a follower of Jesus Christ. Baptisms involve water in one way or another. Sometimes a person gets *submerged*, which means their whole body goes under water. Other times, the new Christian has water gently sprinkled on their head.

Either way, the water is a symbol of washing away the old way of life. It shows how a person is cleansed before they begin their new life as a Christian. Baptisms are so special. Some people are so happy they cry during baptisms. Whether you are the one watching the baptism or the one being baptized, baptisms make your heart and soul feel pure.

Let's talk about your baptism.

(If applicable, pull out photo albums and reminisce. If your child has not been baptized yet, make plans for the day of your child's baptism in the future including clothes to wear, family to invite, and festivities to enjoy afterward)

The day of your baptism was (or will be) so special. The ceremony happened (or will happen) at church. It was (or will be) so important to have our church family there to watch and witness the whole thing. Everyone prayed (or will pray) for you!

(Discuss more details of your specific church's way of performing baptisms, as well as other churches' baptism traditions you've witnessed)

Let's act out your baptism with this bucket of water (or in the bathtub).

In the name of the Father,

(Sprinkle water on your child's head, or prepare to immerse your child in the water)

In the name of the Son,

(Sprinkle water on your child's head, or prepare to immerse your child in the water)

In the name of the Holy Spirit,

(Sprinkle water on your child's head, or help prepare to immerse your child in the water)

Amen!

(1. Sprinkle water on your child's head, or help your child be immersed in the water)

(2. Play in the water together. And, of course, never leave your child unattended in the water)

Can you see how important the water is in the baptism? It makes you feel clean. It makes you feel pure. It washes away the old ways of life without Jesus. It prepares your heart for the new ways of life you will have with Jesus. The water surrounds you and welcomes you into God's family, your church family, and all of Christianity.

Do you know who else was baptized?

(Let your child answer)

Jesus was! It was such a special day! Immediately after Jesus was baptized, "heaven was opened, and he saw the Spirit of God descending like a dove and alighting on him. And a voice from heaven said, 'This is my Son, whom I love; with him I am well pleased'" (Matthew 3:16–17). God was so happy for Jesus.

How beautiful that must have been, to see heaven and hear God's loud and loving voice. I guess that is why every baptism at our church is so special. God is there opening up the heavens, sending his Spirit to rest on us, and feeling well pleased with us as we are cleansed and welcomed into his kingdom. Every baptism can remind us of Jesus' baptism, renew our own baptisms, and help us feel closer to God himself!

Week 13:
The First Disciples

BIBLE READING: Matthew 4:18–22

Dear Parent,

The goal of this week's lesson is for your children to learn about disciples and their influence. A disciple is more than just one of Jesus' students and more than just one of his dear friends. Jesus' disciples are those who carried the message and teaching of Jesus beyond his death and out into the rest of the world. May your children grow in faith and become disciples of Christ.

Materials:

Bible, dominoes

Script:

There are so many people in this world who Jesus wanted to teach about God's love.

Let's pretend this domino is Jesus.

(Pick a domino and let your child hold it)

Jesus can help this one person by teaching him or her.

(Place the Jesus domino vertical on the floor, table, or another flat surface. Then place another domino behind the Jesus domino. Tap the Jesus domino and let it fall into the other one, to make the second domino fall)

Did you see that? Every person Jesus comes across can be affected by his teaching. Every person can feel God's love. Sometimes Jesus taught one person at a time, like we just saw with the dominoes. At other times, Jesus had many people listening to him in the streets, in the temple, or even just sitting on the side of a mountain. In those places, Jesus could reach more than one person at a time with his words.

Let's say one day there were six people listening to Jesus teach about God's love. Now, let's say this one domino is Jesus, and these six are the people listening.

(Make a neat line of vertical dominoes, about seven tiles long. Check that the dominoes are spaced appropriately so that, when the time comes, your child can tap the first one [the Jesus domino], and it will fall into the second, which will fall into the third one, and so on)

Let's see how Jesus teaches and affects people all at once.

(Let your child tap the Jesus domino, and watch the effect together)

Did you see how Jesus affected the people? I imagine they heard Jesus' teachings about God's love and were forever changed.

A time came in Jesus' teachings when he wanted to reach more than just those people who were near him listening. He wanted to reach everyone in the whole world, but he knew it was going to require some help. So Jesus decided to find people he could share his teaching with; then, each of those people could turn around and teach even more people. These chosen people were called *disciples*. Do you know what the word disciple means? It's a person who is learning and following someone's teaching.

Over the years, the disciples went from being regular old fishermen and tax collectors to being the wisest students and helpers in the world, because they got to learn directly from Jesus himself. And then they got to turn around and spread the Word to others!

Jesus started with just two disciples. Their names were Simon, whom he called Peter, and Andrew.

Jesus taught Peter and Andrew about God's love and God's kingdom. Then Peter and Andrew turned around and taught more people about God's love and kingdom! Let's think about this with our dominoes. We have a Jesus domino, but now we need a Peter domino and an Andrew domino.

(Let your child pick out their disciple dominoes. Arrange the line of dominoes so that your Jesus domino will tap the 2 disciple dominoes at the same time. This can be accomplished by placing the Jesus domino in front of $1/3$ of the Peter domino and $1/3$ in front of the Andrew domino. Then, build a line of 6 dominoes directly behind the Peter domino and a line of 6 dominoes directly behind the Andrew domino. Let your child tap the Jesus domino and see the effect on twice as many people)

That was so great! Twice as many people learned about Jesus because of the disciples! Do you know what Jesus did after he found the first two disciples? He found more disciples! He found James and John. He also found Phillip and Bartholomew.

(Play dominoes together. Let the Jesus domino affect the rows behind each disciple domino. Tap the first one in a line at the same time your child taps another line. Emphasize how many can be affected; whereas, without the disciples, only one row of people would have been affected by Jesus' words)

Do you know how many disciples Jesus ended up with before the first Easter? Twelve! Do we have enough dominoes for that?

Probably not! But let's play and try to "teach" as many people about God's love as we can!

You know, you and I are also like disciples, because we're learning about Jesus and turning around to teach others about God and his love every day. We can talk about Jesus to our family and friends. We can teach others just by having Jesus-like behaviors and saying Jesus-like words. Think about how many people *we* can affect. What a blessing!

Week 14: Fishers of Men

BIBLE READING: Matthew 4:18–22

Dear Parent,

Expanding on the theme of discipleship, the goal of this week's lesson is to teach your children how easy it is to become one of them! Jesus' disciples were regular people going about their daily business, but their lives changed drastically because they met Jesus. Some were fishermen who had been "caught" by Jesus' love. And when they decided to become "fishers of men," they spread the gospel and helped others be caught by Jesus' love as well. May we go and do the same.

Materials:

Bible, bucket of water, toy fish, small human-like toy figurines or dolls, and a small net or kitchen colander

Script:

Do you remember what the word disciple means? It's a person who is learning and following someone's teaching. Jesus, the ultimate teacher, needed these disciples to help him teach the whole world about God's love. Do you want to learn more about some of the disciples we talked about last week?

The Bible tells us here in Matthew that Jesus found two of his disciples in a fishing boat! Yes, Peter and Andrew were fisherman before they were disciples.

(Put your hands and your child's hands in the bucket of water, then continue with the script)

Every day before the sun came up, Peter and Andrew woke up and went fishing.

(Put the toy fish in the water and catch them with the net)

Can you try to be a fisherman with the fish in this bucket?

(Let your child try to catch some of the fish)

Good job! You caught some!

(While your child plays, continue with the script)

It was the life of a fisherman to go fishing. If it was sunny, Peter and Andrew fished. If it was rainy, they fished. If it was warm, they fished. If it was cold, they fished. Every day for over twenty years, they fished. Then one day, Peter and Andrew met Jesus by the water, and their lives were changed forever. Jesus saw them in their fishing boat with their father. He called to them, "Come, follow me . . . and I will send you out to fish for people" (Matthew 4:19).

Jesus meant that he wanted the two men to stop spending their time looking for fish to sell at the market. Jesus wanted them to start spending their time looking for people whom they could teach about God's love. And that is exactly what Peter and Andrew did. Peter and Andrew became disciples of Jesus, and then went to find other people, not fish, to tell them about God's love.

Now let's change our activity. We still have our bucket of water, but now, we too can be "fishers of men"!

(Put the small toy people in the bucket)

Can you catch one with the "net"?

Good job. Let's take a minute to look at these people. Do you see how some of them are kind of just floating around in the water? Some are even sinking! They all look a little lost to me. Do they look lost to you?

As fishers of men, we can find people in any situation, whether floating, sinking, lost, or found. We catch their attention, show them God's love, and help them find their way. Let's try it again!

> *(Continue to play. Catch people. Rescue them. Tell them God loves them. Send them on their way with knowledge and happiness in their hearts because of God's love. While you play, tell stories to your child about how Jesus found you. Or did you have the help of a fisherman-turned-disciple to hold you up, rescue you, tell you about God's love, and send you on your way?)*

Week 15: The Lord's Prayer

BIBLE READING: Matthew 6:5–15

Dear Parent,

The goal of this week's lesson is to help your children begin to develop a prayer life. The power of prayer is real. It saves lives, literally and figuratively. Anyone can pray. Everyone can pray. Whether two years old or 102 years old, prayer brings us closer to our dear Lord and, sometimes, to our fellow prayer warriors. Let's help develop that channel of communication today for your children.

Materials:
Bible, snack, and the attached chart

Script:
When do we pray?

(Let your child answer. Responses will be different depending on your household. If you pray at the times listed below, great job—and keep it up! If you don't pray at the times listed below, it's never too late to start. See what works for your family and try to stick with it. If you forget, don't worry. Every day is a new day, in which new and good habits can be started)

Do we (or can we start to) pray to give thanks for our food? Let's eat a snack now and bless our food.

Do we (or can we start to) pray before bed? It helps us sleep happily and peacefully, doesn't it? Let's pretend to go to bed now and say a goodnight prayer.

Do we (or can we start to) pray sometimes when we see ambulances? Let's pray for an ambulance now and pray for the people inside it.

Do we (or can we start to) pray when our own family and friends need help? Let's pray for someone we know who needs help right now.

Do you know who was really good at praying? Jesus was really good at praying! He spent time teaching people how to pray. He said that when we pray we shouldn't do it out loud on the street corners because we want people to see us. Jesus said, "When you pray, go into your room, close the door and pray to your Father, who is unseen (Matthew 6:6).

Let's try it!

(Go into your child's bedroom and lead your child in prayer. Encourage them to pray. Thank God for this time with your child today)

That was so great! I could feel God's presence when we prayed. It was like he was listening to us! Jesus also said, "And when you pray, do not keep on babbling like pagans, for they think they will be heard because of their many words. Do not be like them, for your Father knows what you need before you ask him" (Matthew 6:7–8).

So God already knows what we need. And we can still tell him anything! You can tell him about your day. You can tell him how your heart is feeling at any moment. You can talk to him about protecting our family. You can ask him to help people in need.

In the Bible, Jesus teaches a special prayer too. We call it the Lord's Prayer. It has some words that adults might know better than kids do, but we can break it down together to see exactly what it all means.

(See Table 1. Read the Lord's Prayer, translating each part into kid-friendly language)

A PARAPHRASE OF THE LORD'S PRAYER (MATTHEW 6:9–13), IN VERBIAGE CHILDREN CAN UNDERSTAND.

The Lord's Prayer	What it means to me . . .
Our Father	Dear God,
in heaven,	in heaven,
hallowed be your name,	your name is so holy and awesome.
your kingdom come,	I am glad to be a part of your kingdom.
your will be done	I trust your plans . . .
on earth as it is in heaven.	on earth and in heaven.
Give us today our daily bread.	Please give me food and your daily goodness.
And forgive us our debts,	Please forgive me for when I make bad choices.
as we also have forgiven our debtors.	Please help me forgive others who make bad choices.
And lead us not into temptation,	Please help me to make good choices.
but deliver us from the evil one.	Please keep me safe from harm.
For thine is the kingdom,	I pray to you in your name,
the power, and the glory forever.*	in your strength, and in the joy you give forever.

*The final sentence does not appear in Matthew, but is a doxology traditionally added to the end of the prayer.

I love that prayer. It helps me feel closer to God. Regardless of what we choose to pray for on any given day, it's wonderful and important to spend time with God. Next time I pray, I am going to thank God for prayers and for listening to us today!

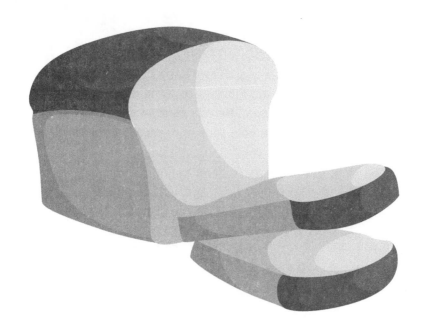

Week 16:
Ask, and It Will Be Given

BIBLE READING: Matthew 7:7–11

Dear Parent,

The goal of this week's lesson is to teach your
children to expand the scope of their praying to
include relying on Jesus. He is there whenever we
have a need or request; all we have to do is ask.
Scripture says that we, as parents, are not the only
ones providing for our children. God provides, and he
often provides through us.

Materials:

Bible, a door in your home—preferably one that doesn't lock (If it
does lock, plan to position your child on the side without the lock), a
slice of bread, a stone, a toy fish, and a toy snake

Script:

Jesus is such a wise man. I love to read the Bible and think about some of the things he has said. Here in Matthew 7:7, Jesus says, "Ask, and it will be given to you; seek and you will find; knock and the door will be opened to you." So I am going to sit on this side of the door. You can sit on that side of the door *(double check that there's no lock on your child's side)*, and we can act out Jesus' words!

(Close the door)

Are you ready to knock? Okay. Go ahead and knock.

(Once your child knocks, open the door and continue with the script)

Hello! Do you see how easy that was? You knocked, and I opened the door. That is what praying to God is like. You say, "Dear God," and he immediately opens the door to heaven in order to listen! Isn't that wonderful?

Let's do it again.

(Close the door. Repeat as many times as your child would like to. Keep emphasizing that God is there waiting. Let your child know that connecting with God is even easier than opening a door)

That was fun. When we look back at that same part of the Bible, we can see what Jesus said next. He said, "For everyone who asks receives; the one who seeks finds" (Matthew 7:8).

So, basically, if we want to ask God for something, we can. Let's try it!

(Close the door)

Are you ready? Now knock, and ask God to keep us safe while we are learning today.

(Once your child knocks and prays, open the door, look around, and continue with the script)

Yes, it looks like we are safe while we are learning today. That was so great! We made a request to God, and he granted it!

When we pray, we do have to be careful what we ask for. It says in the Bible that we shouldn't test God or ask for things he might not have planned for us. But I know with my whole heart that when we make reasonable requests that are within his plans, God can open the door, hear us, and answer our prayers.

Let's see what the Bible says next. Jesus asks, "Which of you, if his son asks for bread, will give him a stone? Or if he asks for a fish, will give him a snake? If you . . . give good gifts to your children, how much more will your Father in heaven give good gifts to those who ask him!" (Matthew 7:9–11).

Do you want to try it?

(Close the door)

Now this time, knock, and ask me for a slice of bread.

(Open the door after your child has knocked and asked)

What do you think? If you are hungry and ask me for bread, will I, your parent, give you this stone? I will not! I love you so much. If you ask for some bread, I will give you some bread. Let's eat it together right now.

(Enjoy your snack together and continue)

Jesus said that if your parent can give you some bread, you will be amazed how much more God can give you if you're in need.

Let's try Jesus' second example.

(Close the door)

This time, knock, and ask me for some fish.

(Open the door after your child has knocked and asked)

What do you think? If you ask me for fish, will I, your parent, give you this snake? I will not! I love you so much. If you tell me you want some fish, I will give you some fish. So again, Jesus said if a parent loves their child enough to give them what they need . . . God loves us even more and can provide for us even more! He is God!

Do you want to play the game some more?

What kinds of things might you ask for . . . ?

77

(If your child would like to keep playing, decide upon and then retrieve more things to ask for. You may want to retrieve something that your child didn't ask for. For example, if your child asks for a spoon, you could give him or her toothpaste to illustrate that God sometimes knows what we need more than we do. Most importantly, enjoy the time together, all the while emphasizing that God will open the door, listen to your prayers, and provide)

Week 17:
Build Your House on the Rock

BIBLE READING: Matthew 7:24–27

Dear Parent,
    The goal of this week's lesson is to show your
children that God is our solid foundation. He is
strong. He is steady. When we build our lives with
him as our foundation, we can withstand anything.

Materials:

    Bible, small blocks, a flat rock, two 9 x 13 baking pans, a plastic
bag filled with sand (a few cups is plenty), a watering can, straws

Script:

    I love to build things. Do you like to build things? Have you
ever tried to build blocks on something soft and mushy like carpet
or grass? It's almost impossible, isn't it? The carpet or grass is just

so unsteady, and when you try to build the blocks higher, they all fall down.

When you build with blocks, it's important to have a solid base or foundation, right? Let's step outside and see what our home is built upon.

(Go outside together and inspect the base of your house, apartment building, etc.)

Look at the very bottom of our home. Our home is built on cement. Cement is made out of hardened rock. So our home isn't going to budge next time it rains or the wind blows really hard.

Jesus had an opinion about how people should build their homes and their lives. Jesus said you should build your life on God just like you would build your house on a strong rock. If you start with God as the basis for all that you do, you will have a sturdy and strong life and home.

Jesus said,

> Therefore, everyone then who hears these words
> of mine and puts them into practice is like a wise
> man who built his house on the rock. The rain came
> down, the streams rose, and the winds blew and
> beat against that house; yet it did not fall, because
> it had its foundation on the rock. But everyone who
> hears these words of mine and does not put them
> into practice is like a foolish man who built his house
> on sand. The rain came down, the streams rose, and
> the winds blew and beat against that house, and it
> fell with a great crash. (Matthew 7:24–27)

Jesus was so wise! Let's act out his wise words with our blocks and materials.

Let's use this flat rock as the foundation for our house. Let's put the rock in this dish so that we don't make too big of a mess. Now we're ready to build with our small blocks. Can you push on this rock and feel how really strong and firm it is? This rock is like our God. This block house is like our lives. We are building our lives on God.

(Continue to build until the structure is complete)

Okay. Let's see if our house is strong because of what it is built on. Let's pour water on it . . . to pretend the rain is falling.

(Gently pour the water to make sure the house stays secure)

Yes! The house is still standing. Now let's pretend there's a flood by pouring more water around the rock. Yes, our little house and our little lives are still standing! It's time to take our straws and blow a wind against our house with our breath.

(Join your child in gently blowing on the house, through straws)

How wonderful! Our house and our lives withstood the rains, the floods, and the winds! Our solid foundation is our God, and he really does make our homes and lives stronger!

Do you want to see what happens when we don't take Jesus' advice? Let's pretend we aren't building our houses and our lives on God. Let's put the sand in this container and try to build.

(Struggle with the building blocks. Allow them to fall because of the unsteady base you are using. After a few minutes, balance the blocks on each other without actually interlocking the pieces. The structure should be very fragile for this part of the lesson)

Wow, this isn't very easy to build this time. Our foundation is all shaky and unstable while we are trying to build our houses and lives. It's no wonder Jesus said we shouldn't build our lives on things that aren't strong. I can barely keep our little house and little lives standing. Now, let's see what happens when the rain comes . . .

(Pour water over the house, allowing the blocks to fall)

Now let's see what happens with the flood.

(Pour a lot of water into the sand in the container. The sand should become more and more displaced)

81

Now let's add the wind.

(Blow together through straws. By now, the house should be demolished)

So what do you think? Do we want to build our houses on the rock or on the sand? Yep, I agree. I think we want to build our house on the rock! We want to build our lives on God. They will both be stronger and able to withstand anything!

Week 18:
The Parable of the Sower

BIBLE READING: Matthew 13:1–9

Dear Parent,
    The goal of this week's lesson is to show your children the different ways to grow. This parable contains metaphors relating to realistic hardships. Yet we learn that when we are in the "good soil" we can grow to be our best, to feel the "light," and to receive our nourishment. We can thrive and produce great things.

Materials:

    Bible, an outdoor area to talk and play, seeds, toy birds, rocks, handful of dirt, one healthy plant with healthy leaves and visible roots, one prickly or thorny plant (or weed), rich and dark soil, and a piece of fruit

Script:

I am so excited about today's lesson! We get to go outside to enjoy our Bible story! Do you know who was a great storyteller? Jesus was! Today, we're going to talk about one of his stories called "The Parable of the Sower."

So what is a "sower"? Well, when it is spelled s–o–w–e–r, it means someone who plants seeds and wants them to grow into healthy plants, which make great fruit. God is like a sower in some ways. He plants seeds of goodness in us, and he wants us to grow into wonderful people, who do great things.

In this story, the sower, or God, scatters seeds in many different places. The first few seeds land on a path; before they can grow, some birds come along and eat them.

> (Act out each step of the parable with the materials listed above. Spread seeds onto a sidewalk or path; use the toy bird to snatch them up)

Isn't it sad that those seeds were snatched up so fast? They won't grow up to be great or even have a chance to make great fruit!

Let's talk about the second group of seeds from the sower. These seeds land on some rocky ground.

> (Sprinkle the handful of dirt onto the rocks. Then put the seeds on top of the dirt and rocks)

There was a little bit of dirt there. But when the seeds started to grow in the dirt on the rocks, there was no depth for their roots to grow. Let me show you about how important roots are on this healthy plant here. Do you see its roots? Roots grow deep into the ground and are where the plant take in water and plant vitamins, or nutrients, from the soil.

Back to the story. If a plant can't grow roots, it won't be good, and it won't produce fruit, will it? Because without water and nutrients, a hot day will come along, with a blazing sun, and the little plant will just burn right up because it never got what it needed from having roots in the soil.

The third place the sower scattered his seeds was among the weeds and thorns.

(Put some seeds next to the prickly weed)

This isn't a good place either, is it? No, it will have trouble getting sunlight for its own leaves through all the leaves of the other weeds. AND, if it tries to grow up higher to get more sunlight, it might get stuck in the thorns. So the little plant will get choked out, right?

Gosh, where is the best place to plant these seeds? I know that God scatters seeds in good soil too.

(Show the rich and dark soil to your child)

Look at how rich and deep this soil is. This is the best spot for the sower to scatter his seeds.

Here, the seeds can push down roots to get the water and nutrients needed. Here, the seed can grow into a plant and can get the sunlight it needs. Here, the plant will continue to grow and produce fruit.

Now if God is the sower and we are his seeds, where do we want to be scattered to grow?

(Let your child answer)

Yes, we want to be in the good soil! We want to push down our roots and get living water from Jesus. We want to grow to reach more light from God. And we want to grow to bear fruit, which means to do great things.

So while you are growing up, don't put yourself in a place to get snatched away by birds or bad choices. Don't try to grow where you shouldn't, like on rocky ground where you can't put down roots or get the things you need to grow. And Jesus' story also teaches us that you don't want to try to grow right next to bad ideas or influences, like those weeds. They'll keep you from reaching the light or keep you from growing with their thorns.

You, *(insert your child's name)*, keep growing in the good soil. Here, you are refreshed by the living water that is Jesus. Here, you can feel God's light as bright as sunshine. Here, you'll grow to do great things in this world . . . and you'll help many other little seeds learn to grow in the same way. I am so proud of how you are growing so far! Let's keep growing together.

Week 19:
The Faith of the Mustard Seed

BIBLE READING: Matthew 13:31–32

Dear Parent,

The goal of this week's lesson is to show your children that, despite their size, they can have the greatest faith in all the world.

Materials:

Bible, one mustard seed (located in the spice section of the grocery store, but if one cannot be found, use one grain of salt as a substitute), one green bean seed (or almost any other larger seed that can be found), and access to window or outdoors to look at a tree

Script:

Look at this seed right here. It's called a mustard seed. Isn't it so small? Do you think this mustard seed grows into a little plant, or a giant bush? Let's think about that for a bit. Look at this green bean seed. It is bigger. Do you think this green bean seed grows into a little plant, or a giant bush?

(Lay the two seeds side by side)

Well, Jesus knows a lot about everything, including seeds. In the Bible, he said:

> The kingdom of heaven is like a grain of mustard seed, which a man took and planted in his field. Though it is the smallest of all seeds, yet when it grows, it is the largest of garden plants and becomes a tree, so that the birds come and perch in its branches. (Matthew 13:31–32)

So, according to Jesus, the tiniest seed can grow into the largest tree in the garden. In fact, this mustard seed will grow to be so much bigger than this green bean seed, which at most will grow to be two feet tall. It is not the size of the seed that counts; it's the kind of growth and the development that determines its size.

Jesus' words make me think about you and about your faith, which is how much you believe in God.

How big are you? Are you smaller than me? Are you smaller than your teacher? Are you smaller than our neighbor? Are you smaller than a firefighter?

(Let your child answer)

Yes, but how big is your faith? How much do you believe in God?

(Let your child answer)

Your faith is huge! And I know your faith can grow as big or bigger than anyone else's in the world. I know your faith can be as big, strong, and solid as a tree.

I see your faith is growing. It's getting bigger every week. I can't wait to see how big you and your faith grow from here!

(Look out the window, or go outside and look at a tree together. Talk about how small they started out and how big they got. Remind your child that each one started with one small seed . . . Just like our faith. Faith in Jesus causes all kinds of growth, possibilities, and new heights)

Week 20:
The Leaven Parable

BIBLE READING: Matthew 13:33

Dear Parent,

The goal of this week's lesson is to appreciate, together with your child, how God's love changes us. Without God, we would be something entirely different than we are with God's love. We would feel incomplete and unsatisfied, rather than fully developed and truly blessed.

Materials:

Bible, flour, a spoon, and a loaf of bread. If you have the time and desire, bake bread together using a recipe with yeast, warm water, flour, salt, sugar, and oil. If not, simply set out some of the bread ingredients during the lesson to reinforce the message.

Script:

Some of my favorite parts of the Bible are Jesus' teachings. He is so wise. One day, he tried to tell people how God's love really changes them. Without God's love, we would be like this flour here. Let's examine it together.

(Look at it together with each of your senses, and notice all the properties of the flour)

It looks fine, when I look at it closely.
It smells fine, when I sniff near it.
It feels fine, when I touch it.
Let's see how it tastes.

(Taste it together)

Yuck! Was that delicious and wonderful to you? Not to me either. I guess it wasn't delicious because it is just flour . . . not a whole loaf of bread. Since flour is just one ingredient, it stands alone; it is small, and it is incomplete.

However, when we add other ingredients together with the flour, we can make a whole loaf of bread. Let's taste the bread.

(Taste it together)

Yum! That's delicious and wonderful!

I guess the flour and bread are a lot like us. If we were alone without God's love, we would stand alone, we would be small, and we would definitely be incomplete. But when we are added together with God's love, we evolve into something wonderful too!

So, whether we are talking about adding other ingredients to flour, or about God's love being added to us, we both turn into something bigger, something more wonderful, something that fills you up and satisfies a hunger. Praise God for his love!

Week 21:
The Lost Sheep Parable

BIBLE READING: Matthew 18:12–14

Dear Parent,

The goal of this week's lesson is to play out the loving and inspiring parable of the lost sheep. We all feel lost at times, whether we're two years old or one hundred and two. Knowing this parable at a young age is critical. It helps us, when we feel lost, to truly know God is searching for us, and he will prevail in finding us. Once found, we can rest in knowing God loves us, and he will always keep us safe.

Materials:

Bible, one hundred small toys or objects, and, preferably, at least one small sheep

Script:

Look at all of the materials for our Bible playtime today! How many items do you think we have here?

(Let your child count as high as they can. Then finish counting together)

We have one hundred small items here! Let's imagine that all of these items are sheep.

Do you know what a group of sheep is called?

(Let your child answer)

A group of sheep is called a flock. We can spread out our flock right here as if they are sheep grazing on grass near a mountain. Will you help me set out ninety-nine of the "sheep"?

Now we still have one sheep left over, don't we? Let's imagine that this little sheep is lost. I will put it away from the flock and out of sight.

Jesus used to tell a story about a big flock of sheep. Do you want to hear it?

(Let your child answer)

Jesus said,

> If a man owns a hundred sheep, and one of them wanders away, will he not leave the ninety-nine on the hills and go to look for the one that wandered off? And if he finds it, truly I tell you, he is happier about that one sheep than about the ninety-nine that did not wander off. In the same way your Father in heaven is not willing that any of these little ones should perish. (Matthew 18:12–14)

Isn't that wonderful? In this story, Jesus is trying to tell us that God is the shepherd!

(If necessary, explain what a shepherd does)

Jesus is also trying to tell us that each one of us is like one of his sheep!

(Point to one of the sheep in the flock)

Jesus wants us to know that if we ever feel lost in life, that God will search for us, find us, love us, and keep us safe.

I want to play a game. Can you close your eyes for a minute? Please don't peek!

(Hide the one "sheep" that you set aside earlier)

Now open your eyes. Let's pretend you are the shepherd, also known as God, and you will work hard to find your one lost sheep.

(Let your child find the sheep. Give hints if necessary. Celebrate together once your child finds the sheep)

You did wonderful! We searched for the sheep. We found the sheep. We love the sheep and will keep it safe! It's exactly like Jesus' story! Let's play again!

(As you play, reiterate the teaching point)

Just like a sheep can be lost on a mountain, a person can feel lost in life. What are some ways that we could feel lost?

(Let your child answer)

If we do something wrong, we could feel lost. If our feelings get hurt, we might feel lost. If we forget to pray for a few weeks, we might feel lost. If any of these ever happens and we do feel lost, we just need to remember that we are just like the sheep in Jesus' story! God will search for us. God will find us. God loves us and will keep us safe!

Can we play again? Why don't *you* hide the lost sheep this time? I'll pretend to be God, and I will search for it, find it, love it, and then keep it safe.

Week 22:
Jesus Heals Two Blind Men

BIBLE READING: Matthew 20:29–34

Dear Parent,

The goal of this week's lesson is to help "open your children's eyes" to Jesus. Jesus had the power to heal the sick. He fed the poor. He gave sight to the blind. When you stop to think about it, he does the same things for us every day. He heals us, nourishes us, and lets us "see" the truth that only he provides. Let's demonstrate this to your children.

Materials:

Bible, a closet or other darkened room, flashlight, snack, two blankets, two pillows, paper and crayons, small bag to put the materials in.

(Take a few extra minutes to familiarize yourself with the script, since you will be in the dark for the majority of the lesson)

Script:

Do you know what it means to be blind?

(Let your child answer)

Right! It means you can't see well, and, in some cases, you can't see anything at all. That would be a big change, right? I love to see things. I love to see your face. I love to see the pictures you draw. I love to see the sunset. It would be difficult to not be able to see anything. But if we were blind and unable to see, our bodies would adapt to make up for the lack of sight. And, luckily, today there are tools to help blind people live well and have normal lives.

However, a long time ago, during Jesus' time, blind people did not have any tools to help them. Back then, if they couldn't see anything, they couldn't do anything. That would be a very hard way to live. Let's try to understand what that might feel like.

Let's go to the darkest room in our house. Ready? Let's go.

(Go to the dark room, and bring your materials with you)

Here we are. Let's sit down. I'm going to turn off the light now. Ready?

(Use your flashlight if you must in order to read the script or find one of the materials, but encourage your child to keep their eyes closed. Your child will better understand the lesson while immersed in darkness)

It is really dark in here. I can't see anything. And yet, I know it's snack time. How are we going to be able to eat without being able to see. Let's try. Otherwise, we'll be hungry. Where is our snack? Let me feel around in this bag with my hands. I can't see it, but I can try to feel the shape of it.

What kind of snack is it? We can't see it, but we can try to smell it. Can you tell what it is? Now let's aim for our mouths and try to eat. This eating without being able to see isn't easy. Can you imagine eating like this three times every day?

Next, let's try to take a nap. Where is my blanket? Where is yours? Where is my pillow? Where is yours? Ouch. When I laid down, I kicked something in the corner. This is tricky not being able to see! Can you imagine getting settled in your bed like this every night?

Next, let's try to draw a picture. Let's see if we can get our crayons and paper. Can you draw a flower or a fish? This is hard! I wonder what the picture will end up looking like!

Not being able to see is *really* affecting us! With help from family and friends, and with time to help our other senses adapt, things would get easier. But I have even more respect for blind people now. They overcome hardships daily that I hadn't thought about.

In our Bible story today, there are two blind men sitting on the roadside. Let's keep our lights off and imagine how those two blind men feel. The two blind men can't see, but they hear the excitement of Jesus coming. They begin to yell out to him, "Lord, Son of David, have mercy on us!" (Matthew 20:30).

I'm sure they knew about some of the miracles Jesus had performed. I'm sure they knew how special and amazing Jesus was. They must have been thrilled to find out that Jesus was going to be walking by!

Then Jesus spoke to them, "'What do you want me to do for you?' he asked. 'Lord,' they answered, 'We want our sight'" (Matthew 20:32–33). Jesus touched their eyes, and they immediately could see everything around them.

(Turn on the light)

Isn't it wonderful? Look at everything around us! Think about the two blind men being able to see for the first time! Jesus gave the gift of sight to the men! Jesus works miracles!

I also like this story for another reason. Without Jesus' love, it would be hard to see anything, whether or not our eyes are blind. But through Jesus, anyone and everyone can see the greatest love in the world! Jesus didn't just open the blind men's eyes for them to see. He opens their hearts for them to see the greatest love in the world!

Week 23: The Parable of the Wedding Feast

BIBLE READING: Matthew 22:1–14

Dear Parent,

This week's lesson will enlighten your children about the kingdom of heaven, using the parable of the wedding feast. As in so many of his parables, Jesus uses engaging comparisons to reveal the true nature of his kingdom to us. This "wedding feast" (fellowship with God in his kingdom) has been magnificently prepared by the "king" (our God). The king has invited every one of us. The "invitation" (Jesus' love and sacrifice) must be accepted for entrance into the feast. And as Jesus says in this parable, "For many are invited, but few are chosen" (Matthew 22:14). We have complete freedom to respond or to not respond to his gracious invitation into eternal life. Enjoy this time, and make sure your children understand that today is about more than a feast. May you talk, share, and accept the Lord's life-changing invitation.

Materials:

Bible, wedding pictures of parent, family member, or friend, pencil, six small sheets of paper, six plates, six napkins, six cups, silverware for six, a pitcher filled with water or juice, toy food or real snacks, a candle, and music (optional)

Script:

Have you ever been to a wedding?

(Discuss with your children if and when they attended a wedding)

Weddings are so very exciting. It is the joining of two people together in marriage. It is all about celebrating love. Let's look at some wedding pictures together.

(Look at the pictures and try to point out the ceremony as separate from the reception)

After the wedding, there is usually a gathering to celebrate. It is called a reception or a feast!

Jesus talked about a wedding feast in the Bible. He said the kingdom of heaven is like a wedding feast planned by a king for his son. Do you want to hear about it? Let's pretend to have a feast here as we learn about what Jesus said.

First, the king sent out invitations. Let's make some invitations too. Let's write, "Big and Fancy Wedding Feast! Please come!" on each one. How many should we make? The king probably made hundreds, but, with our little hands, let's just make six. Great! Let's pretend that we sent them out.

(Put them in a mail box or outside the door)

Next, we should start getting things ready. Just like the king! It is time to set the table. We need plates, napkins, silverware, and cups. We can fill this pitcher with water and pour a little in each cup too. We should also put food on each plate. We can even light a candle and put on some music, if you want.

(Have fun setting a special table with your child)

Finally, we are ready!

Jesus said that, after all the work was done, the king was ready too. The dinner was prepared, and the drinks were poured. Then the king began to wait for the guests.

(Wait quietly. Look at the clock. After a minute, resume the script)

You won't believe this, but in Jesus' story, no one came to the king's feast! The people who were invited didn't accept the invitation to come. But look at this wonderful wedding feast! Think about the magnificence of the king's feast. We worked so hard; the king and his servants worked so hard! I can't believe no one came, can you? Do you want to know what the king did next?

Jesus said the king told his servants to "go to the street corners and invite to the banquet anyone you find" (Matthew 22:9). And the servants did just that. They invited everyone. They invited people who made good choices and people who made bad choices. Any and all were invited to come.

I am happy to say that the wedding hall became filled with guests. I bet it was such a wonderful feast. When you read the story in the Bible, you'll see that it turns out to be a great and happy story.

I know why Jesus told this story. He wanted to help us understand how much God wants us to be with him in his kingdom. God is like the king! He invites everyone to be with him and to enjoy all the wonderful things he has, just as the king in the story invited everyone to the feast. In the story, the king sent invitations. In life, God sent us an invitation by sending his son, Jesus.

The doors to God's kingdom aren't open for just anyone to walk in. *Everyone* is welcome, but we have to accept Jesus in order to enter the kingdom of heaven, just like the people in the story had to accept the king's invitation to enter the feast. I am so happy God invited me to live with him forever in his kingdom. In fact, I am so happy, I'm accepting the invitation of Jesus' love. How about you?

Week 24:
The Greatest Commandments

BIBLE READING: Matthew 22:34–40

Dear Parent,

The goal of this week's lesson is to go deeper and yet simplify the commandments. We discussed the Ten Commandments several weeks ago, including how impossible it is to follow every single one of them every single day. That is where Jesus comes in. He could obey every commandment, and he did. And when he died for our sins, he made a true sacrifice of himself for us. But before his crucifixion, Jesus summed up the Ten Commandments for us. He said, "Love the Lord your God with all your heart and with all your soul and with all your mind. This is the first and greatest commandment. And the second is like it: 'Love your neighbor as yourself'" (Matthew 22:37–39). What a blessing to have every sermon, every rule, and even the entire Bible simplified into these loving instructions.

Materials:

Bible, your child's favorite color paper, a heart-shaped stencil or a heart drawn freehand, scissors, markers, and tape

SCRIPT:

Do you remember a few weeks ago when we talked about God's rules? Do you remember how many of them there were?

(Let your child answer)

Yes, there were ten! Can you remember some of them?

(Let your child answer)

It's okay. It is hard to remember every single one of them, isn't it?

Well, if we can only remember one or two every single day, wouldn't it help us to know which ones are most important? Who would know the answer to that question?

(Let your child answer)

Jesus knows the answer! In fact, a man asked Jesus about it a long time ago. Aren't we glad he asked? Let's find Jesus' answer in our Bible.

(Read Matthew 22:35–39 to your child)

That is wonderful! Now we know that, if we do nothing else each day, we need to at least try to follow those two commandments.

Let's make reminders and tape them to the bathroom mirror. Then when we brush our teeth in the morning, we will remember the two most important rules. *And,* when we brush our teeth at night, we can ask ourselves how we did and pray to do even better tomorrow!

So let's make two hearts and write what Jesus says are the greatest rules on them.

(Use the materials to make two hearts)

We can now write, "Love God with all your heart, soul, and mind." Hmm, what does this mean exactly? If I love God with all my heart, I can put my hand on my chest and feel warmth from my heart. My heart gets its warmth from the love I share with God.

Next Jesus says we need to love God with all our soul. That one is not as easy to feel with your hand. Loving God with our souls can be felt through prayer. If we focus on talking to God and getting that clear connection between us down here on earth and him up there *(point down to your child and up to heaven)*, then we are more likely to feel our souls loving God. Let's pray, "Dear God, I am loving you right now—with my soul. Please help me feel the strength of this connection between you and me. Amen." Did you feel it? We can keep practicing that one. And with our reminder on the bathroom mirror, we will remember to practice!

Also Jesus says to love God with all our mind. That's easy! Let's just think, "I love God, I love God, and I love God." Are you thinking it with your mind? It would be good to do that one a few times a day.

Great work! Our heart reminder of the greatest commandment is done! Let's make the second heart. What was that commandment again?

(Let your child answer)

Yes, it's Love your neighbor as yourself. Let's write that one down and then think about what it really means. For example, when we see a friend hurting, we should help them because we would want help if we were hurting. When we see a friend who needs something, we should try to get that something for them, because we would want it for ourselves.

> *(Discuss an example in your own life in which you have helped someone—perhaps someone who was hurting or in need of food or clothing. Talk about how that action follows the commandment. Your child would want help if he or she was hurt; your child would want a coat if he or she was cold, for instance)*

What a good example! The second heart is done. Now let's decorate them as we continue to think about them.

Is it time to go hang them up? I hope we can follow them the best we can every single day!

Week 25:
Let the Children Come

BIBLE READING: Mark 10:13–16

Dear Parent,

This week, you and your children will recognize together the progression of faith and love in their hearts. Read today's Scripture and know that you are doing your part in bringing your children closer to Jesus through church, Sunday school, and even working through this devotional. Your children are now within Jesus' reach. And as this week's verses affirm, know that "he took the children in his arms, placed his hands on them and blessed them" (Mark 10:16).

Materials:

Bible, sidewalk chalk, and an outdoor area

Script:

I believe Jesus is right here with us all the time, even though we can't see him. But if he was sitting right here and we could see him with our eyes today, I think I would ask him a question. Of course, I would praise him, worship him, and hug him first. But then I would ask him what his favorite Scripture in the Bible is.

Do you have a favorite lesson that you have learned from this book and from Jesus so far?

(Let your child answer)

Yes, that is a good one. I have lots of favorites.

(Share your favorite lesson or two so far)

But I would imagine that one of Jesus' favorites might be Mark 10:13–16, because it is about children just like you. Let's read it together.

> People were bringing little children to Jesus for him
> to place his hands on them. . . . He said to them,
> "Let the little children come to me, and do not hinder
> them, for the kingdom of God belongs to such as
> these. Truly I tell you, anyone who will not receive
> the kingdom of God like a little child will never enter
> it." And he took the children in his arms, placed his
> hands on them and blessed them.

Jesus loves children. He wants kids to know about him as early on as possible in their little lives. If children know Jesus when they are young, they can feel his love sooner. If they feel his love sooner, they can have a better life earlier.

For today's Bible playtime, let's go outside and look for a cement area that is close to a tree.

(Look together; find a good spot)

We are going to pretend this tree is Jesus. We're going to make paths to Jesus with our sidewalk chalk for all children to come to him directly. Let's start with as many brightly colored paths to Jesus as we can possibly make.

(As you and your child draw, continue with the script)

(Insert your child's name), I know the path you are on . . . and it is leading straight to Jesus.

(Draw another path leading to the tree)

I hope that *(Insert the name of your child's best friend)* is on the path leading straight to Jesus.

(Draw more paths and more arrows "straight to Jesus" for other kids your child names and for children all over the world. Enjoy the activity and your blessed time together)

Week 26:
Centurion's Servant

BIBLE READING: Luke 7:1–10

Dear Parent,
    The goal of this week's lesson is to emphasize to
your children that Jesus can do anything. Jesus can heal
the sick. Jesus can also heal those who aren't physically
sick, but are brokenhearted. Jesus can heal all of our
hearts every day with authority, if we just believe it so.

Materials:
    Bible, toy doctor tools (If you don't have them, substitute some
child-safe items from the medicine cabinet in your home, such as
bandages and gauze)

Script:
    Today's lesson is about a centurion. Do you know what that is?

(Let your child answer)

A centurion is a big word that means an important army officer in charge of one hundred people. Now that we know what it means, we can learn about one particular centurion in the Bible.

One day, a centurion asked his friends to go tell Jesus that his servant was so sick he couldn't even move. The centurion believed Jesus could heal his servant. Let's try to imagine what it feels like to be so sick that you can't even move.

(Lay on the floor side by side, as you continue with the script)

Move your foot. Now stop moving your foot. Next, imagine you want to move your foot, but you can't. Okay, move your knee. Now stop moving your knee. Next, imagine you want to move your knee, but you can't. Okay, move your hips. Now stop moving your hips. Next, imagine you want to move your hips, but you can't. Okay, move your belly. Now stop moving your belly. Next, imagine you want to move your belly, but you can't.

Okay, move your hands. Now stop moving your hands. Next, imagine you want to move your hands, but you can't. Okay, move your arms. Now stop moving your arms. Next, imagine you want to move your arms, but you can't. Okay, move your head. Now stop moving your head. Next, imagine you want to move your head, but you can't. Finally, move your whole body. Now stop moving your whole body. Next, imagine you want to move your whole body, but you can't.

It would be sad and scary to be that sick, wouldn't it? When we are sick, what do we do to try to get healed?

(Let your child answer)

Right. Now let's pretend to fix your feet . . .

(Using the toys or other materials you collected for the lesson, continue with all the body parts mentioned previously: feet, knees, hips, belly, hands, arms, and head)

Well, I am glad we had those healing tools, but the centurion believed Jesus didn't need any tools or medicine! The centurion had so much faith, he believed Jesus could heal his servant without healing tools and without even coming to his house to see the servant! He believed Jesus could heal his servant just by saying some healing words out loud in the streets of the city.

The centurion believed Jesus' power to heal was in some ways like his own power as an officer over many soldiers. The centurion said to Jesus,

> Say the word, and my servant will be healed. For I myself am a man under authority, with soldiers under me. I tell this one, "Go," and he goes; and that one, "Come," and he comes. I say to my servant, "Do this," and he does it. (Luke 7:8)

Basically, the centurion was saying to Jesus, if you say out loud for him to be healed, he will be. Jesus was so happy to hear that the centurion believed strongly in him and his power to heal. Then Jesus did heal the centurion's servant.

Jesus wants all people to believe that strongly in him. Do you believe in Jesus that strongly? I do! I just know Jesus can do anything! He can heal the sick. He can heal those who aren't sick, but have broken hearts. He heals our hearts every day with authority, if we just believe it to be so.

Week 27: The "Good Neighbor" of Samaria

BIBLE READING: Luke 10:25–37

Dear Parent,

This week, you'll dive deeper into Jesus' greatest commandments—to love the Lord our God, and to love our neighbors as ourselves. But who are our neighbors? How can we love them? Although it's important to set parameters with our children about who they can safely help and how, it is never too early to start helping them grow compassionate and Christ-like hearts.

Materials:

Bible, adhesive bandages, markers, and small stickers: crosses, hearts, stars

Script:

Do you remember when we talked about Jesus' greatest commandments? We put the reminders for them on our bathroom mirror, right? Can you remember them?

(Let your child answer)

"'You shall love the Lord your God with all your heart and with all your soul and with all your mind.' . . . And the second is like it: 'Love your neighbor as yourself'" (Matthew 22:37–39).

That verse makes me wonder, *who is my neighbor?* Who do you think our neighbors are?

(Let your child answer)

A neighbor is anyone who lives next to you, yes. But a neighbor can also be anyone you come across at any point during the day. For example, in Jesus' mind, my neighbor is *(name someone you came across yesterday—a bank teller, mail delivery person, teacher, or just someone you simply passed along your way. It would help the lesson if your examples are people your child might remember seeing as well).*

Here's a story in the Bible, one Jesus told to help us recognize who our neighbors are:

> A man was going down from Jerusalem to Jericho,
> when he was attacked by robbers. They stripped him
> of his clothes, beat him and went away, leaving him
> half dead. A priest happened to be going down the
> same road, and when he saw the man, he passed by
> on the other side. So too, a Levite, when he came to
> the place and saw him, passed by on the other side.
> But a Samaritan, as he traveled, came where the man
> was; and when he saw him, he took pity on him.
> He went to him and bandaged his wounds, pouring
> on oil and wine. Then he put the man on his own
> donkey, brought him to an inn and took care of him.
> The next day he took out two denari and gave them

118

to the innkeeper. 'Look after him,' he said, 'and when I return, I will reimburse you for any extra expense you may have." (Luke 10:30–35)

So, which one of these three was a good neighbor?

(Let your child answer)

Yes, and Jesus said, "Go and do likewise" (verse 37).

Let's look at these bandages here. These help us when we have an injury, right? Whenever you have a cut or a scratch, I put one of these on it, don't I? Well then, I must love you, my neighbor, as myself just as Jesus instructed.

Let's decorate these bandages with cross stickers and heart stickers and stars, to remind us to love and help our neighbors when we see that they're hurting.

(As you enjoy decorating the box of bandages, keep discussing the lesson)

Do you remember when *(insert the name of someone who was recently injured and needed a bandage)*? Did I just walk on by? No! I helped and did everything I could to help my neighbor feel better. I loved my neighbor as myself.

Now, you're a kid, so you might not always have bandages right there with you when you're at school or Sunday school. But if a neighbor does get hurt on the playground, you can go get help. Finding a teacher or other adult who can help is like going to get a bandage from the cupboard . . . and loving your neighbor as yourself.

There are other ways people can be hurt and other ways we can help. Can you think of any?

(Let your child answer)

Sometimes we come across neighbors who are having a sad day at school or Sunday school. You might be able to help them. Your kindness can be like a bandage to their heart . . . and loving your neighbor as yourself. Your prayers can be like a bandage to their heart . . . and loving your neighbor as yourself.

(Continue to discuss examples of helping, but also reinforce your family's safety parameters)

I sure hope our neighbors don't get hurt any time soon. But the next time we pull out these bandages from this box, we will smile. It will be a great reminder of Jesus and his commandment to love our neighbors as ourselves!

Week 28: The Prodigal Son

BIBLE READING: Luke 15:11–32

Dear Parent,

The goal of this week's lesson is to show your children how God is our ever-loving and ever-accepting Father. We, as humans, make mistakes and bad choices, whether by accident or on purpose. Whenever we ask for forgiveness and seek to bring ourselves closer to God, he will always be there with arms wide open to greet us and celebrate our "coming home."

Materials:

Bible, party decorations (streamers, blowers, balloons), robe, dress-up jewelry and shoes, and snacks

Script:

While Jesus was alive and preaching God's Word, everyone wanted to be with him: rich people, poor people, young people, old people, people who made good choices, and people who made bad choices. Everyone wanted to be with Jesus.

Some people, watching all of the activity, were surprised Jesus was nice and welcoming to *everyone*. Tax collectors, who were not always honest at their jobs, were accepted by Jesus. Jesus also accepted all sinners. Sinners is a word used to describe people who make bad choices very often. Eventually, the people watching asked Jesus how he could accept the "bad" people just as easily as he could accept the "good" people. Jesus responded by telling them a story to help them understand.

In Jesus' story, there was a man with two sons. The youngest one asked for his share of his father's money. When he received it, he made bad choices. He took the money, left home, and spent it all. The young son became sad. He also became hungry and homeless. His bad choices left him with nothing. After a long time passed, he decided to return home to his father's house.

Back at home, the father could see his youngest son walking toward the house from a long way off. He ran to his son, hugged him, and kissed him. The son told his father he was so sorry for making bad choices. The son also asked for a job in order to be able to buy food. In having his son back, the father was not mad at all. In fact, the father's response was very loving!

The father said, "Quick! Bring the best robe and put it on him. Put a ring on his finger and sandals on his feet. . . . Let's have a feast and celebrate" (Luke 15:22–23).

(As you dress for the feast, continue with the script)

Although the youngest son had been gone for a time, now he had come home! He used to make bad choices, but now he wants to make good choices! And the big party was underway.

So today let's have a party in honor of the youngest son too. He was lost, and now he is found. He has come home! We should decorate with streamers, blow our horns, and celebrate coming home to our Father . . . who is God! Let's celebrate the change in the youngest son's heart and anyone else's heart, whenever they decide to come home and make good choices from now on!

(As you decorate, continue with the script)

Jesus told this story because the father in the story is like God. The youngest son in the story is like the tax collectors and sinners Jesus was so kind to . . . or even like you and me when we make mistakes. Jesus wants us all to celebrate whenever people who have been making bad choices start to make good ones—whenever anyone "comes home" to God and his love!

(Enjoy celebrating together)

Week 29: Zacchaeus' Change

BIBLE READING: Luke 19:1–10

Dear Parent,

The goal of this week's lesson is to show your children that knowing Jesus can change how we live. As we discussed last week, a person can go on making bad choices for years. But once that person finds Jesus, every day thereafter can be better. Every good choice can be a little easier to make. Knowing Jesus transforms us from the inside to the outside. It starts in our hearts, progresses to our soul, and then the mind begins its own transition. From there, new and good actions and reactions are inevitable. This is a wonderful miracle: a relationship with Jesus changes our hearts!

Materials:

Bible, broom, nine quarters, and any money-related toy items, such as a piggy bank, cash register, play money from a board game, calculator

Script:

In the Bible, we can read about a man named Zacchaeus. Zacchaeus was the chief tax collector in the city of Jericho. Zacchaeus was a very important man because he held the top position of all the tax collectors. He had to make sure that when the people in Jericho earned money for their work during the day, they gave some of it to the city.

People in Zacchaeus' time had to work hard to earn money, just like we still do today. So let's try to understand what Zacchaeus did for his job as a tax collector. Here is a broom. Let's pretend that you live in Jericho, and your job is cleaning floors.

(Go to any uncarpeted floor, and help your child use the broom to sweep. Talk to your child about hard work and earning money. Continue with the script)

Good job on the floor! Let's say you earned five quarters for that hard work. Here you go.

(Count out five quarters and give them to your child)

Now, if your daily job was cleaning the floors, Zacchaeus' daily job as a tax collector was to come by and take some of your money. So even though Zacchaeus didn't sweep the floor, he would come over and order you to give him two of your five hard-earned quarters.

That may not seem fair, but tax collecting is how a city, or even a country like the United States, earns money to function. However, if Zacchaeus was like a lot of tax collectors in Jericho during that time, he would go ahead and give the government one of your quarters. But do you know what he did with the other quarter? He would sneak it into his pocket and keep it.

Was that a good choice? No, it wasn't. Was that fair to the person who worked so hard to earn it? No, it wasn't. Was that fair

126

to the city who needed the tax money to function? No, it wasn't. Can you believe that Zacchaeus did this to everyone who lived in Jericho? So he was a very rich man but not well liked. He must have had so much money. Let's play with this money and imagine how much Zacchaeus may have had.

(Play together. Count and sort the money. Then, set the fortune of Zacchaeus aside)

Let's get back to the Bible story. One day, Zacchaeus found out that Jesus was coming through his town. He wanted to see Jesus, and he wasn't the only one. There were crowds of people waiting to see Jesus.

Now, Zacchaeus was not a tall man. He really did want to see Jesus, but he couldn't see through or over the crowds. So do you know what he did? He, the chief tax collector, climbed up a sycamore tree in order to see Jesus! When Jesus came near the area of the tree where Zacchaeus was, Jesus looked up and told Zacchaeus he wanted to spend the day at Zacchaeus' house. Zacchaeus came down and greeted Jesus happily.

After spending a day with Jesus, Zacchaeus' heart changed. He told Jesus, "Look, Lord! Here and now I give half of my possessions to the poor" (Luke 19:8).

(Look at the fortune you and your child have been imagining belonged to Zacchaeus. Help your child divide it in half, and talk about Zacchaeus' transformation)

Can you believe it? Zacchaeus wanted to give to others half of everything he had gotten for himself. Now that he was friends with Jesus, he wanted to help people, and he didn't want to steal from them anymore. What a wonderful change!

Do you know what else Zacchaeus said? He said, "And if I have cheated anybody out of anything, I will pay back four times the amount" (Luke 19:8). That is quite a promise. So do you remember that one quarter we imagined Zacchaeus taking from you after you swept the floor? Now let's imagine Zacchaeus came back and gave you that quarter and four more quarters!

(Count out four quarters and hand them to your child. Talk about all the people who would be getting four times the amount of money they'd been cheated out of. Set those monies aside for those imaginary people so that your child can see what is left in the fortune)

Let's see how much money might be left in Zacchaeus' fortune. Hmm. A lot less! But I think Zacchaeus didn't care how much money he had left. He had Jesus in his heart instead, which made him richer and happier than he would have been with all the money in the world.

Zacchaeus underwent a huge change. As we grow in Jesus, our hearts, souls, and minds undergo a change too. Naturally, through this process, our actions and even our lives will change . . . for better, and for good!

Week 30:
The Woman at the Well

BIBLE READING: John 4:1–26

Dear Parent,

The goal of this week's lesson is to help your children better understand Jesus' love. There are many similarities between Jesus' love and water. Some of the resemblances are literal; some are figurative; some are just plain inspiring. Like water, Jesus' love has the ability to fill us up. Both have a cleansing nature. Both are necessary for growth. Both have the potential to overflow, and to lift us off the ground. And both can be poured out onto all of us.

Materials:

Bible, a room with a faucet and drinking water, two cups, two large buckets, swimsuit, and either a hose in a backyard or bathtub in a bathroom

Script:

What do you do when you are thirsty and want some water?

(Let your child lead you to your home's drinking water source. Fill two cups and drink together)

During Jesus' time, if you wanted water, you had to walk to a place called a well to get it. The well wasn't right outside of your home either. People had to walk a long way to get to the well. Since it was so far away, they would bring buckets with them in order to collect extra water. That way, they wouldn't have to travel more than once a day to the well.

(Walk to the hose or bathtub and fill up the buckets)

Now, try to carry this bucket filled with water. It's heavy, right? Can you imagine how hard it would be to carry both of these buckets back from the well every day? I am glad we have faucets now. But whether water is easy or difficult to obtain, everyone needs it to live.

One afternoon, Jesus was traveling on a long trip. He had walked a very long way. And he still had a long way to go. Jesus stopped at a well, like the one we talked about. He saw a woman filling up her buckets. She was all alone. She hadn't come in the morning, when her friends and neighbors usually did. So it seems as though she may not have had any good friends and neighbors. Regardless, Jesus asked the woman for a drink. The woman didn't know why he would ask her for a drink. They didn't know each other. They were strangers, raised by totally different groups of people.

When the woman asked why, he said, "If you knew the gift of God and who it is that asks you for a drink, you would have asked him and he would have given you living water. . . . Everyone who drinks this water will be thirsty again, but whoever drinks the water I give them will never thirst" (John 4:10, 13).

Can you imagine never being thirsty again? Jesus gives us something that we need every day. He gives us something that is like a kind of water for our hearts and minds. Really, what Jesus gives us is his love. And, just like water, we can't live without it.

Close your eyes and imagine doing what you do every day—getting a drink of water. Now, imagine Jesus standing right there! Imagine Jesus giving you what you need.

(Play in the water. If it is the right temperature, pour it gently onto your child's back and shoulders)

Water can fill you up . . . Jesus giving his love fills you up.

(Pour again)

Water makes you clean . . . Jesus' love makes you feel clean.

(Pour again)

Water helps us grow . . . Jesus' love helps us grow.

(Pour again)

Water overflows . . . Jesus has so much love for us, it overflows our hearts.

(Pour again)

Water makes us feel light and its buoyancy can lift up an entire ship in the ocean . . . Jesus' love makes us feel light and lifts up our spirits.

(Pour again)

Water pours out . . . Jesus' love pours out onto you and me.

Week 31:
Jesus Feeds Five Thousand

BIBLE READING: John 6:1–14

Dear Parent,

This week, you'll try to help your child grasp the reality and significance of Jesus' feeding of five thousand people with simply five loaves of bread and two small fish. What an amazing miracle! The key to fully understanding this miracle is to demonstrate the math involved: the immensity of the crowd; how little food there was to begin with; and the twelve baskets of leftovers. Jesus truly is the greatest miracle worker of all time!

Materials:

Bible, a lunch bag containing five bite-sized crackers and two grapes, and twelve baskets, bowls, cups, or plates

Script:

Jesus was a wonderful teacher. People followed him around every day hoping to hear what he might say or teach. Do you want to know how many people followed him on one special day?

(Let your child answer)

One day, Jesus had five thousand people following him! That sounds like a lot! How many is that?

(Show your child this picture)

Here is a picture of five thousand people. That's a lot of people, isn't it? In today's Bible story, five thousand people had been following Jesus and listening to his teaching for so long that everybody got hungry for dinner. Uh oh! How do you feed five thousand people dinner? Even a whole grocery store wouldn't have enough food for that! And back in Jesus' time, they didn't have grocery stores.

What did Jesus do? Well, Jesus asked his friends to help find food for all the people. One friend named Andrew, who loved Jesus very much, said, "Here is a boy with five small barley loaves and two small fish" (John 6:9). Everyone looked at Andrew like he wasn't making any sense. They knew that wouldn't be enough food for five thousand people! That would be like trying to feed our whole church with just five small crackers and two grapes!

(Eat the snack together)

Did that tiny snack fill you up? It didn't fill me up either. Jesus fed five thousand people with just five loaves of bread and two fish. Somehow Jesus, with all his power and goodness, made that tiny bit of food enough for all those people. The people didn't just eat a little snack either. The Bible says they feasted. Their five thousand bellies were stuffed! And do you know what else? In this miracle, Jesus made the bread and fish into so much food, there were leftovers! The Bible says there were enough leftovers to fill twelve baskets.

(Count out the twelve baskets or bowls, one at a time)

What a miracle! It almost seems like magic, but Jesus, and only Jesus, can make something so amazing happen. Let's go over the math one more time. Jesus started with how much food?

(Let your child answer)

And he gave it to how many people?

(Let your child answer)

And he had how many baskets piled high with leftovers?

(Let your child answer)

Wow! I love Jesus so much. He is the most amazing and giving person that ever lived. Do you think so?

Seasonal Lessons through Easter

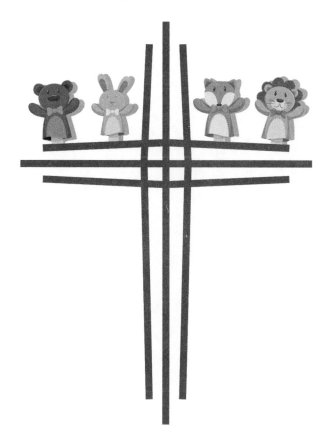

Week 32:
Our Biggest Valentine

BIBLE READING: John 3:16

Dear Parent,

    The goal of this week's lesson is to celebrate love . . . with God. Being a follower of Christ permeates every facet of our existence. We don't have to have separate compartments for separate parts of our lives anymore. Jesus has access to all of us and loves us wholly, which feels wonderful. So celebrate Jesus' love today.

Materials:

    Bible, colored paper, markers, heart stickers, scissors, glue, and doilies

Script:

Do you like Valentine's Day?

(Let your child answer)

I know! I do too! Valentine's Day is a special day to tell the people we love how much we really do love them. I will tell you. You will tell me. We will make some phone calls to tell family members that we love them. We will make valentine cards for friends. It's such a great holiday!

When I think about Valentine's Day, I can't help but think about the one in the universe who loves me the most: God! One of the most famous quotes in the Bible is John 3:16. It reads, "For God so loved the world that he gave his one and only Son."

God loves us so much that he sent Jesus to earth to teach us, love us, and make our hearts clean and perfect. You know what? I feel loved just talking about it.

I am who I am today because of God's love and Jesus' love. And you are here spending Bible playtime with me today because of God's love and Jesus' love. So let's make a valentine for our God who loves us so much that he gave us his only Son. Let's make the prettiest valentine we've ever made! Are you ready?

(Enjoy crafting the valentine together. What a blessing that God can be a part of this holiday and every day)

Week 33: Palm Sunday

BIBLE READING: Matthew 21:1–11; John 12:12–16

Dear Parent,

The goal of this week's lesson is to prepare your children for Easter. The Easter holiday is as significant as Christmas! Think about it; neither holiday would exist without the other. You can't celebrate Jesus' resurrection without the occurrence of his birth. And Jesus' birth would not be so widely celebrated if it wasn't for his mission and ultimate resurrection. This "Holy Week" leading up to Easter begins with Palm Sunday and Jesus' triumphal entry into Jerusalem. Enjoy the lesson as you reenact the parade. Also, enjoy the next few lessons as they lead up to the happiest, most glorious, and most loving day of the year—Easter.

MATERIALS:

Bible, as many small figurines as you can collect—people, princesses, action figures, small toy donkey or horse, at least eighteen napkins or toilet tissue squares, and leaves—one for each figurine you were able to gather

Script:

Have we ever watched a parade together?

> *(Let your child answer. If you have, discuss the details of that day with your child)*

I love to watch parades for holidays. The Thanksgiving Day Parade is *so* fun to watch on TV. It has balloons that are as big as buildings, and hundreds of dancers and singers performing.

Another holiday parade is the Rose Parade on New Year's Day. During that parade, you get to see marching bands and floats. The floats are big moving displays of cartoon characters and animals. The amazing part of that parade is that each float is made up of thousands of flowers. Such a beautiful sight to see!

There are parades to celebrate famous people in history, like Martin Luther King Jr. who wanted everyone in America to get along and act like brothers. There are parades to celebrate champions in sports. There are even parades to celebrate the seasons of the year. Parades are such special celebrations.

Do you want to know which parade is my absolute favorite? The one Jesus was in before the very first Easter! Jesus wanted to make a big entrance into the city. He knew it was going to be a special parade because it was a part of God's plan and a part of the Bible we would read about forever.

I've gotten some toys together to help us imagine what that great parade into the city might look like. So which of these toys or figurines should we pretend is Jesus?

> *(Let your child pick)*

Great! Next, we can pretend these two are the disciples who brought Jesus a donkey to ride (or, if applicable, the horse).

(Act out the remaining portions of the script with the materials you have collected)

After the disciples brought the donkey, they put their cloaks or coats onto the donkey for Jesus to sit on. Wasn't that nice?

(Use a napkin for this task)

At that point, Jesus was ready to start the parade! He started riding the donkey and entered the city gates! So many, many people were there. They saw Jesus coming.

(Line up the figurines in two parallel lines about one foot apart)

As people saw Jesus entering the city, they began to take off their cloaks to make the way nicer and more special for Jesus.

(Lay out the toilet tissue squares in front of the figurines in the line)

While some people spread their cloaks on the road, others gathered palm branches and handed them out to each person in the crowd. Next, everyone started waving their palm branch in the air and saying, "Hosanna to the Son of David!", "Blessed is he who comes in the name of the Lord!", and "Hosanna in the highest heaven!" (Matthew 21:9).

Do you know what *Hosanna* means? It means "save us." And that is truly what Jesus did after the parade and on that first Easter. He saved our lives and helped us become closer to God. Next week, we will talk more about exactly *how* he saved us. But for now, let's give each person a pretend palm branch to wave back and forth.

(Keep playing with the parade as you reiterate the story to your child)

What a wonderful parade that must have been! The palm branches are why we call this day in history *Palm Sunday*. The Palm Sunday parade is important because it celebrates Jesus as God's son. Jesus is the King of all kings. Jesus is the Prince of Peace. Jesus is the greatest person in the whole world because he came to show us God's love. His parade begins Holy Week for our family and our church. His parade begins the chain of events that lead up to Easter Sunday!

Hosanna! Hosanna!

Week 34:
Maundy Thursday, Part One

BIBLE READING: Matthew 26:26–29

Dear Parent,

The goal of this week's lesson is to continue to prepare your children for Easter. We celebrate Jesus' last supper with his disciples many times throughout the year. Every time we take communion or break bread with friends and family, we can do so in remembrance of Jesus Christ. Enjoy today's feast with your child. Easter is coming.

Materials:

Bible, tablecloth, napkins, and dishes (preferably ones used for special occasions), utensils, glasses, small loaf of unsliced bread or rolls, grape juice and red wine (for adults if desired), and confetti hearts, crosses, or any other religious festive table decorations

Script:

Easter is coming up so soon! Isn't that exciting? We should do some more learning about the events leading up to Easter, in order to make sure our hearts are ready to celebrate.

Today we are learning about what happened at a special meal Jesus hosted for the Jewish holiday of Passover. Jesus had celebrated Passover all his life, just like we celebrate Thanksgiving. But he knew this feast would be different than any other time he had celebrated it.

This feast would be Jesus' Last Supper. During this feast, he would tell the disciples about his big plan to save them . . . and to save you and me. Before the feast, which was a few nights before that first Easter Sunday, Jesus began to make preparations. He sent two disciples out to prepare the place where they would eat.

Let's prepare too. We will need some materials to make the table look very special. Like Jesus did, let's make this feast different from every other time we have celebrated.

(Set the table. Decorate the table. Have fun preparing)

It looks lovely! Now, back to our lesson. As Jesus and the disciples were eating, "Jesus took bread, and when he had given thanks, he broke it and gave it to his disciples, saying, 'Take and eat; this is my body'" (Matthew 26:26).

(Thank God for the bread. Break it. Give some to your child. As you eat, continue with the script)

Jesus knew he was going to die the next day. I know that seems like a sad thought. Jesus was and still is the greatest man in the whole wide world, and you might be thinking that you don't want him to have to die. I understand. I felt the same way at one point too. But you can see Jesus' love in his death, and in this bread.

By giving the bread to us and saying it is "his body," Jesus showed that he gives his life for us. In fact, that's the whole reason he was born on Christmas Day. Jesus was going to grow up, live perfectly, and then give himself for us. Taking the bread *(or crackers, depending on your church's practice)* at church and at home is a great reminder of Jesus' giving, isn't it?

Next, Jesus "took a cup, and when he had given thanks, he gave it to them, saying, 'Drink from it, all of you. This is my blood of the covenant, which is poured out for many for the forgiveness of sins'" (Matthew 26:27–28).

(As you drink, explain . . .)

Just like he poured from the cup, Jesus was going to pour himself out. He was going to give himself, to take the punishment for our mistakes. Jesus knew that we, as humans, are not perfect enough to be close to the awesome, almighty God on our own. No matter how hard we try, we are going to make mistakes, which are also called sins. So when Jesus gave the cup, he gave us his perfection. We can now be close to God because, after taking the cup, God no longer sees our mistakes when he looks at us. God sees Jesus' perfection and our love for Jesus.

Jesus wanted to save us, and he showed us that with the bread. Jesus wanted to give us his perfection, and he showed us that with the cup. Now, every time we break bread, every time we eat bread, and every time we drink from a cup, we can thank Jesus for giving himself for us. It's the greatest love anyone has ever known.

Week 35:
Maundy Thursday, Part Two

BIBLE READING: John 13:1–5

Dear Parent,

Let's continue to prepare for Easter and revel in the cleansing power of Jesus! We hear the words "forgiveness of sins" all the time, but when was the last time we stopped to visualize what that looks like? Today, you will demonstrate it for your children in the same way Jesus did for the disciples at the Last Supper. You might just enjoy the reminder too.

Materials:

Bible, a large bowl of warm water, soap, and towel

Script:

Do you remember when we talked about the bread and the cup at that very special feast? Well, on that same night, Jesus did something else to show his love for the disciples and for us. Jesus washed his disciples' feet!

It sounds funny, and I know you're thinking it should be the other way around, but that is the beauty of the story. So let's think deeper about it all. Most people back then did not have shoes, and if they did they probably wore something that looked like today's flip flops. Imagine walking around all day in the desert or the city with flip flops on! Regardless of where they walked, the disciples' feet must have been covered with dried dirt and dust! Well, listen to what Jesus did next:

> Jesus knew that the hour had come for him to leave
> this world and go to the Father. . . . so he got up
> from the meal, took off his outer clothing, and
> wrapped a towel around his waist. After that, he
> poured water into a basin and began to wash his
> disciples' feet, drying them with the towel that was
> wrapped around him. (John 13:1–5)

That sounds like a dirty job! Jesus, the greatest man in the world, did the dirty job that was usually done by servants. But he wanted to show the disciples his love and also his new promise . . . by cleansing their feet.

Think about the mistakes and sin we talked about in the last lesson. Those things that we do wrong might make us look dirty to God, right? Those mistakes and sins are the things that keep us from being clean and perfect, right? So it would also be those same mistakes and sins that keep us away from God. We couldn't get near the great Almighty God while we were dirty and imperfect; that is, until that first Easter weekend when Jesus changed everything.

By washing the disciples' feet and dying on the cross, Jesus was showing the disciples how he could make the them clean. He cleaned their feet in the wash basin to show them that he would clean their hearts when he was on the cross.

Jesus did the hard job of cleansing them in order to bring them closer to God. And what Jesus did for them is the same thing he does for us. Jesus washes away the mistakes and sin from our hearts as easily as washing the dirt off our feet.

Let's look at your feet from today. Yes, they look dirty to me! This dirt on your feet is like the mistakes you made today. Do you remember when you *(insert an example or two of the mistakes your child made today. For example, "Do you remember when you disobeyed mommy today while we were at the grocery store?" "Do you remember when you said something to your brother that wasn't nice?" "Do you remember when you didn't clean up your toys when I asked you the first time?")*

Well, none of us are perfect. And these are the kinds of mistakes that keep us from being perfect, right? And any mistake makes us look dirty to God and keeps us from being close to him, right? Yes, until that first Easter weekend, because Jesus washed them away!

(Wash your child's feet as continue with the script)

Jesus makes you clean! Jesus cleans your heart as completely as I am washing your feet! Jesus knew you couldn't be perfect on your own, but he knew that he was! He knew by washing away your mistakes and sin he could make you clean in God's eyes. He knew he could bring you closer to God if he cleansed you by paying for your mistakes.

(Dry your child's feet as you say . . .)

Jesus is so amazing. His love is unlike anything in this world. Should we wash my feet too? Oh, goodness, my feet are dirty too. I wasn't perfect today either. You may not have realized this, but I . . . *(insert an example or two of the mistakes you made today. For example, "Do you remember when we were driving to the grocery store? Well, I had a not-nice thought about another driver.")* These are the kinds of mistakes that keep me from being perfect. And they make me look dirty to God, and keep me from being close to him. But then, Jesus washes my mistakes away too!

(Wash your feet as you continue with the script)

Jesus makes me clean! Jesus cleans my heart as completely as we are washing my feet! Jesus knew I couldn't be perfect on my own, but he knew that he was! He knew by washing away my mistakes and sin he could make me clean in God's eyes. He knew he could bring me closer to God if he just cleansed me by paying for my mistakes.

(Dry your own feet, and continue to give thanks to Jesus for his sacrifice)

This cleansing shows us the greatest and truest love in all the world. Jesus loves us that much.

We are one day closer to Easter and the celebration of our Jesus who saved us.

Week 36: Good Friday and the Resurrection

BIBLE READING: Matthew 27:43–54 and 28:1–10

Dear Parent,

The goal of this week's special lesson is to help your child visualize Jesus' resurrection. His body lay in the tomb, and then it didn't. It is a miracle and the foundation of our entire faith.

Materials:

Bible, tent or a pretend "cave" made with blankets, and a big beach ball

Script:

Easter might be just one day of the year, but we can celebrate it every day of the year. This holiday is so very important. During the last lesson, we talked about Jesus' love for us, how he cleanses us, and how he gave his life for us. But what does "He gave his life for us" mean?

Sometimes it's hard to think about, but Jesus actually died while he was here on earth. His body stopped living; his mouth stopped breathing; his heart stopped beating. It was a sad day. Jesus never did anything wrong, and yet, he was punished and hung up high on a cross to die.

It used to make me want to cry when I thought about it. Then I learned that Jesus didn't just die. *He died for us!* Jesus was willing to take the punishment for all of the mistakes and sins done by you and me and the whole world. It was his mission and purpose . . . to give his life for us. That is what happened on the day we call Good Friday. Good Friday is an interesting name for the day Jesus died, isn't it? It might be called Good Friday for the good and amazing thing Jesus did for us.

Let's go inside our tent now and talk about what happened next. On Good Friday, Jesus' body, which was no longer breathing, moving, or living, was taken off the cross and placed in a cave called a *tomb*. We can pretend this tent is that cave or tomb. Jesus' tomb had a big boulder in the front of it so that no one could get in or out.

> *(Lead your child out of the tent, close it, and roll the ball in front of it)*

People mourned Jesus on Good Friday evening and all day Saturday as well. Jesus' disciples and friends really missed him and wondered what they were going to do without him. On Sunday morning, Easter morning, a friend and follower of Jesus' named Mary Magdalene decided she would go see the cave where his body lay. She was so sad, and she missed Jesus. When she arrived, there was a huge earthquake.

> *(Shake the tent)*

Then an angel came down from heaven and rolled back the stone!

> *(Roll the beach ball or "stone" away)*

The angel sat on the stone. He looked as white as lightning and snow. The angel said to Mary Magdalene, "Do not be afraid, for I know that you are looking for Jesus, who was crucified. He is not here; he has risen, just as he said. Come and see the place where he lay. Then go quickly and tell his disciples: He has risen from the dead" (Matthew 28:5–7).

Mary Magdalene went inside the tomb. She could see it was empty. Jesus was not there! Jesus died for her and for all people on Good Friday; then, he had risen on Easter! Jesus was alive again!

Let's go into our cave-like tomb too. We can see it is empty, isn't it? Jesus is not here! Jesus died for us on Good Friday and has risen on Easter! Jesus is alive again!

In the Bible, we read that Mary Magdalene left with great joy to tell others the good news. Do you want to know who met up with her on her way? Jesus himself—alive, breathing, and real! Can you imagine how Mary Magdalene felt?

First, she had been crying because she missed her sweet Jesus. So, she had gone to where his lifeless body was supposed to be lying. Next, she saw an angel. After that, she saw the empty tomb. And then, she saw Jesus! The saddest day turned into the happiest day in the world!

I'm so glad you know why we celebrate Easter. Jesus overcame death. Jesus has risen. Easter is a miracle and a blessing. I love Jesus! And Jesus loves me!

Week 37: Easter

BIBLE READING: Matthew 28:5–7

Dear Parent,

It's Easter! Celebrate with your children! For thousands of years, people have celebrated springtime with flowers, baskets, and eggs to hunt. Some of your own fondest memories might take place on an Easter morning. Oh, the joy of finding an egg and putting it in a basket is thrilling! At the same time, it's important to keep the resurrection of Jesus at the center of any ritual or tradition surrounding Easter. What is the point of finding an egg if we haven't found Christ? Today's lesson may become a new addition to your family's yearly celebrations.

Materials:

Bible, several hard-boiled eggs, an egg decorating kit, cross stickers (or waterproof tape cut into the shape of a cross), crayons, basket, and a paper heart

Script:

I'm so happy! We are celebrating Easter! It's the best day of the year! It's a day we celebrate Jesus! We celebrate Jesus' love for us! We celebrate how Jesus gave his life for us and for our mistakes! We celebrate how Jesus brings us closer to God! And we celebrate how Jesus is stronger than anything—even death! Oh, there is so much to celebrate!

When we think of Easter, we sometimes also think of Easter eggs.

(Show one of the eggs to your child)

Eggs always make me think of new life. They can make us think of new life because they are where baby chicks come from, right? And really, Easter eggs can make us think of new life because Jesus is not dead anymore and he became alive again on Easter! Another reason Easter eggs might make us think of new life is because Jesus offers us the gift of new life through his death on the cross for us. Jesus offers us a new life that is closer to God.

Why don't we decorate these eggs together with crosses and things Jesus likes? Then these eggs will go from being just regular old eggs to special eggs, decorated to celebrate Jesus' new life and the new life Jesus gives us.

(Decorate together)

Now that our "Jesus eggs" are done, the other thing we need for our activity today is a heart. A heart is a symbol of love. We have hearts in our bodies, and we fill them up with love from God, Jesus, parents, family members, and friends. We need to put this paper heart in the bottom of a basket.

Are you ready to have a hunt? I will hold the Jesus eggs and you can sit on a chair with your "heart basket." Close your eyes. No peeking! We are going to have a "Jesus is in my heart" Easter egg hunt!

(While your child's eyes are closed, hide the Jesus eggs in various places around the room)

Are you ready to find the Jesus eggs and put them in your heart basket? Great! So instead of saying, "Find the egg and put it in the basket," we are going to say, "Find *Jesus* and put him in your *heart.*" Won't that be fun?

(Play together. Encourage your child with phrases like, "Find Jesus and put him in your heart!", "Can you find Jesus?", "Do you have Jesus in your heart?", and "Put more Jesus in your heart!"

Enjoy the hunt together)

Post-Easter
Lessons

Week 38: Doubting Thomas

BIBLE READING: John 20:19–31

Dear Parent,

The goal of this week's lesson is to help your children know they can believe in Jesus sight unseen. In many cases, seeing does not solely lead to believing. We can feel Jesus' presence and know he is with us every day.

Materials:

Bible, blindfold, and a bag filled with a ball and a small pillow (optional additions to bag: lollipop, cup, and sheet of paper)

Script:

Today, we are going to talk about something that happened after Jesus became alive again. After that first Easter, Jesus went back to see his friends, the disciples. "[He] said to them, 'Peace be with you! As the Father has sent me, I am sending you.' And with that he breathed on them and said, 'Receive the Holy Spirit'" (John 20:21–22). Isn't that amazing? I would love to feel that Holy Spirit coming straight from Jesus' breath! Let's imagine how good that felt!

(Blow on each other's faces)

On that night, one of Jesus' disciples was not there. His name was Thomas. By the time Thomas arrived, Jesus had already left. The other disciples excitedly told Thomas that Jesus was alive, and that he'd come to visit.

Unfortunately, Thomas did not believe his friends. He said, "Unless I see the nail marks in his hands and put my finger where the nails were, and put my hand into his side, I will not believe" (John 20:25). How sad that Thomas didn't believe Jesus was living again!

I wasn't there to see Jesus that day, but I believe Jesus had risen and was alive again. I believe he was there with his disciples. Do you believe?

(Let your child answer)

Thomas must have been awfully sad because he couldn't believe what he couldn't see. Do you want to know what happened next? Jesus showed up again! He appeared to Thomas and said, "'Peace be with you!' Then he said to Thomas, "'Put your finger here; see my hands. Reach out your hand and put it into my side. Stop doubting and believe" (John 20:26–27).

Next, Jesus said something so beautiful. Even though he said it way back then, he was speaking to all Christians for all time, including you and me. He said, "Blessed are those who have not seen and yet have believed" (John 20:29).

I believe. I haven't seen Jesus' face, but I know he is real. Here, let's put this blindfold on you while we learn about believing and not seeing.

(Get the ball out of the bag and put it in your child's hands. Ask your child to identify what it is. If needed, help your child figure out that it's a ball. Take the blindfold off)

How did you know it was a ball? You couldn't see it, but you could feel it, couldn't you? That is how it is with Jesus. Even though you can't see him, he is real. You can feel him and know he is here with you. Do you want to try again?

(Put the blindfold back on your child. Place the small pillow in your child's hands. Ask your child what it is. If necessary, help your child figure out that it's a pillow. Take the blindfold off)

How did you know it was a pillow? You couldn't see it, but you could feel it, couldn't you? Again, that is how it is with Jesus. Even if you can't see him, he is real. You can feel him and know he is here with you.

(Play as many times as you want using a lollipop, a cup, a sheet of paper, or other items. Reiterate the point of the lesson: Even when you can't see him, Jesus is real and he is with us)

Week 39:
Jesus is the Bridge

BIBLE READING: John 14:6

Dear Parent,

The goal of this week's lesson is to help your children "bridge the gap." Through your teaching and the lessons, your children have learned so much. They now know that without Jesus' sacrifice, we would never be able to reach God. Jesus truly is our path and our bridge—the only way to get to God. He paved the way from where we stand to the glory of God's presence. With this lesson, your children will be able to better understand Jesus as the "the bridge."

Materials:

Bible; enough blocks to build two separate towers; items to decorate one tower (stickers, string, coins); anything that is flat, long, and narrow that can be used as a "bridge" (perhaps a piece of toy race track or a book); one large figurine to represent God; one small figurine to represent your child

Script:

After celebrating Easter, we have a greater understanding of what Jesus did for us. We talked about how Jesus washes away our mistakes just like he washed the disciples' feet. We talked about how Jesus gave his body and his blood for us, just as he passed the bread and the cup.

Today let's take a step back and look at the big picture. We can see where God is, where we are, and where Jesus is. Let's build a tower. Let's make it awesome. It will be God's tower.

> *(As you build, talk to your child about God's almighty power, his huge presence, his all-knowing existence, and his awesome influence. Enjoy building together. Make the tower as wide and as grand as possible. Decorate God's tower together. Place the figurine that represents God on his tower)*

God's tower turned out so great. It represents heaven and God's place in the universe. It is where our awesome God stays.

Now let's build a tower for us. Our tower won't be quite as fancy as God's, will it? No, we might work hard and try hard, but our tower will never be the same as God's.

> *(Make sure the tower is tall enough to be connected by the "bridge," but less wide and less decorated; this will help distinguish heaven from earth. Put your child's figurine on this tower)*

Look at our tower. It's nice, but we can't reach God's tower from ours. Can we? No. Well, that makes us separate from God. The thought of being separated from God in heaven forever would make me sad. Would it make you sad if you were separated from God and didn't know how to change it?

> *(Let your child answer)*

Do you know what, or rather, *who*, can change it? Who is the only one that can fix our separation from God and bring us closer to him? Jesus is the only one! Yes, he is perfect. Yes, he is God's son. Yes, he comes from God. Yes, he is also fully human. And most importantly, he is our bridge! Jesus said, "I am the way and the truth and the life. No one comes to the Father except through me" (John 14:6).

(Use the toy or track or book to bridge the gap)

The only way for us to get to God is through Jesus. Jesus is the one who brings us close to God. Jesus bridges the gap between our human mistakes and a whole eternal life with God. Jesus is the one who died for our sins and made us clean enough to pass over the bridge to our God in heaven.

(Allow the figurine that represents your child to move across the bridge to get to God. Let both figurines play together and celebrate their togetherness!)

Thank you, Jesus!

Week 40: The Ascension

BIBLE READING: Acts 1:6–11

Dear Parent,

   The goal of this week's lesson is to teach your children about Jesus' ascension to heaven. Jesus was born here on earth. After his resurrection, he spent time here on earth. And the Bible says he will return to earth again. So where else does Jesus reside today? Jesus is in all sorts of places, as we will see this week with the Ascension and next week when we teach your child about the Holy Spirit. For now, let's focus on what Scripture reveals in the miracle and mystery of Jesus' ascension to heaven. It is a great account for us to remember and share. Jesus truly is everywhere.

Materials:

Bible, four balloons filled with air (not helium)

Script:

Where do you think Jesus lives?

(Let your child answer)

I can think of several places where he lives. He lives in my heart. He lives in your heart. He is above us to watch over us. He is below us to lift us up when we feel down. He is beside us to be our best friend. He is *everywhere.*

I think of another place when I think about where Jesus lives: heaven! Do you want to hear about one of the times he went there? Well, a long time ago, after his resurrection on Easter, Jesus was talking to his disciple friends. They were asking Jesus a lot of questions. They wanted to know when God was going to do this and when God was going to do that.

Jesus told the disciples that only God knows when certain things will happen in this world. And right when Jesus said those words, he was lifted up off of the ground, and a cloud took him out of everyone's sight!

While the disciples were gazing upward, two angels said, "why do you stand here looking into the sky? This same Jesus, who has been taken from you into heaven, will come back in the same way you have seen him go into heaven" (Acts 1:11).

That's amazing! Can you imagine that while you're having a conversation with Jesus, he's lifted up into heaven right before your eyes? We have a few things to play with today to help us envision what that would look like. Let's take these balloons and throw them up as high as we can.

(Play with your child, swatting balloons up high over your heads)

Do you see how they go up? Now can you see how they come back down to us? Just like Jesus, these balloons can go up to heaven and back down to earth. Do you see how lovely and graceful the balloons can be! Jesus is lovely and graceful too. Let's do it again and again. Jesus is so awesome! He can be up in heaven and here with us. Jesus is everywhere! Praise God!

172

Week 41: The Holy Spirit

BIBLE READING: Acts 2:1–4

Dear Parent,

The goal of this week's lesson is to introduce your children to the third member of the Trinity, the Holy Spirit. It might seem like a more difficult concept to teach young children, but it can be done. To be effective, you will want to examine your own memories for instances in which you clearly felt the Holy Spirit. Have you ever stood on a mountain and felt the wind on your face? The Holy Spirit was there. Have you ever held a newborn baby and felt its freshness from God? The Holy Spirit was there.

Keep in mind that the Holy Spirit is not just around during our most magnificent moments. It can be felt on an ordinary day: when sunlight shines through a window and gives you warmth, or during times of prayer. It can be found in the midst of heartbreak or sadness. When pain turns into comfort, and comfort turns into peace, God's presence in the form of the Holy Spirit was there too. So before this lesson commences, find time to reflect on your personal experiences of the Holy Spirit, and let it guide you today.

Materials:

Bible, electric fan, pinwheel or small flag, and bubbles

Script:

Have you ever heard of the Trinity?

(Let your child answer)

Well, God has three parts. The first part is God the Father, and we sure know about him! He is in charge of the whole world! The second part is Jesus, and we have learned a lot about him this year! He is God's son, the one who gave himself for us and is our bridge to God. Today we are going to talk about the third part of the Trinity. We call it the Holy Spirit. It will be fun to learn about. But you will have to pay attention because we can't see the Holy Spirit, we can't hear it, we can't smell it, and we can't taste it. We sure can feel it though.

In the Bible, the Holy Spirit was felt for the first time during a feast called Pentecost. Jesus, and some people who believed in him, were "all together in one place. Suddenly a sound like the blowing of a violent wind came from heaven and filled the whole house where they were sitting. . . . All of them were filled with the Holy Spirit" (Acts 2:1–4).

That must have been so magical! To be gathered with friends somewhere and all of a sudden feel the Holy Spirit. It must have felt like a breath of heaven.

They didn't have fans like ours back during Bible times, but they wouldn't need one if they felt that violent rushing wind! Let's imagine we are there. We can use our fan. Let's turn it on, close our eyes, and let air fill the room.

(Do more than go through the motions together. Really stop, listen, and feel. Without turning off the fan, continue with the script)

You know, I have felt the Holy Spirit before.

(Pull out the pinwheels or flags. Play together and discuss. Share as many instances as you can while your child is still playing and listening. The more you share, the more they will understand that the Holy Spirit is real. If needed, use the examples in the "Dear Parent" note at the beginning of the lesson)

Now that you know what the Holy Spirit is, think back through your young life; was there ever a time you could feel it?

(Let your child answer. Dip the bubble wand in its solution. Let your child hold it in front of the fan so that it blows bubbles through the air)

I am so excited to think about your whole life ahead of you. There will be so many times that you will feel the Holy Spirit. It will be like having God all around you during the greatest moments of your life. It will be like having God with you in prayer. It will also be God's way of being there to help you on your sad days.

(If so moved, you can say, "You know what, this is such a wonderful moment with you that I can even feel the Holy Spirit right now")

Week 42: Peter Heals

BIBLE READING: Acts 3:1–10

Dear Parent,

The goal of this week's lesson is to help your children grasp Peter's wise words, "Silver or gold I do not have, but what I do have I give you" (Acts 3:6). No matter who is ailing, or what the hardship, there is hope, and there is help . . . in the name of Jesus Christ.

MATERIALS:

Bible, two dolls or small stuffed animals

Script:

Two of Jesus' disciples were walking up to their temple, which was like a church. They were walking to the temple to pray, when they came upon a man who hadn't been able to walk since he was born. For as many years as the man had lived, he had to be carried everywhere he needed to go. These days we have tools to help people who can't walk, but back in Bible times those kinds of tools weren't available. Let's imagine what that feels like to be carried everywhere you need to go.

Now, sit down and pretend your legs don't work. If you are hungry, you will have to ask someone to lift you up and carry you to the kitchen.

(Lift and carry your child to the kitchen)

If you are tired, you will have to ask someone to lift you up and carry you to your bed.

(Lift and carry your child to bed)

If you have to go to the bathroom or to brush your teeth, you will have to ask someone to lift you up and carry you there.

(Lift and carry your child to the bathroom)

I know I do still carry you sometimes. But you are still small, so it isn't too much trouble. But let's imagine that *(insert the name of a grown man that your child knows, such as a parent, grandparent, uncle, or neighbor)* can't walk. So if he gets hungry, we will have to find a way to carry him to the kitchen. If he is tired, we will have to find a way to carry him to his bed! If he has to go to the bathroom, we will have to find a way to get him there! What a hard life for a grown man with legs that don't work! And what a hardship for the people around him who need to help him all day.

Well, this man in the Bible whose legs didn't work was outside the temple. The man asked Peter and John for money, which he probably needed to buy food, since he couldn't work at a job because of his legs. Do you know what wise Peter and John said to him? They said, "Silver or gold I do not have, but what I do have I give you. In the name of Jesus Christ of Nazareth, walk" (Acts 3:6). Peter took the man by the hand and helped him up. Right then, the man's legs were strong and healed! He stood on his own! He walked! And he leaped! And then he praised God!

All of the people in and around the temple recognized the man as the one who always sat outside the temple asking for money because his legs didn't work. Everyone was so surprised and happy for him. His problem was solved! Jesus helped him through Peter and John!

No matter what problem you come across, Jesus Christ can help through others and through you! You might not have silver and gold, but what you have you can give to others. So in the name of Jesus Christ, help them!

Let's imagine this baby doll has a problem.

(Pick up the first doll)

Let's say this baby doll is a real person, and she is sad because someone was not nice to her at school. That would be a hardship and a real problem, right? Well, guess what? You can help. You might not have silver and gold, but what you do have, you can give to others. So in the name of Jesus Christ, help her! You can help her by asking her to play or by drawing a picture to make her smile. Let Jesus heal through you! No problem is too big for Jesus!

Now, let's imagine this doll has a problem.

(Pick up the second baby doll)

Let's say this doll isn't doing well in school. Let's say he is supposed to know all of his letters before kindergarten starts, and he doesn't. He is sad and worried. Well, guess what? You can help. You might not have silver and gold, but what you do have, you can give to others. So in the name of Jesus Christ, help him! Offer to sing the alphabet song together or practice your letters with him. Let Jesus heal through you! No problem is too big for Jesus!

Many times in life you will need to help others. At other times, you might realize that you are the one who needs help. Either way, we can be thankful for our lesson today. You can always try to remember: You might not have silver and gold, but what you do have, you can give to others. So in the name of Jesus Christ, help them!

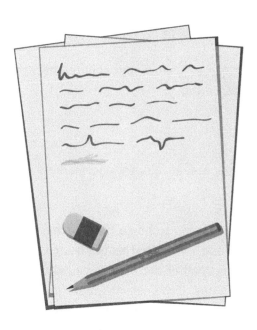

Week 43: Paul's Letters

BIBLE READING: Acts 9:1–19

Dear Parent,

The goal of this week's lesson is to talk about Paul's letters. Paul's perspectives on Jesus' teachings are integral to our faith. For example, anyone who has ever attended a wedding has probably heard, "Love is patient, love is kind. It does not envy, it does not boast, it is not proud. It does not dishonor others, it is not self-seeking, it is not easily angered, it keeps no record of wrongs. Love does not delight in evil but rejoices with the truth. It always protects, always trusts, always hopes, always perseveres" (1 Corinthians 13:4–7).

These loving words are just a taste of Paul's wisdom, written in letter form to the first Christ followers. Written to us. Paul's influence on the early church as well as today's church has been

monumental. Let's show your children how they can
have influence too.

Materials:

Bible, pencil, papers, envelopes, and markers

Script:

Today's lesson is going to be so fun. Come look at the Bible
with me. It's a big book, isn't it? This big book is made up of lots of
little books. The first half of the Bible is called the Old Testament. It
talks about God's plans, God's lessons, and God's history, starting
with the beginning of time and finishing before Jesus was born. The
second half of the Bible is called the New Testament. All of these
little books talk about God's plans, God's lessons, and his stories,
starting with Jesus' birth and finishing at the end of time.

Several people helped to write out the lessons and stories in
the Bible. One of those people was Paul. At first, Paul didn't know
Jesus. For a long time, he walked around with an angry heart. But
then Paul's life changed. He saw a bright light from heaven and
heard the Lord's voice call to him. Jesus asked Paul why he was so
angry and instructed Paul to "go into the city, and you will be told
what you must do" (Acts 9:6). Paul was so shocked. He went to
the city and waited. He couldn't see, eat, or drink for three days,
probably because he was so surprised that Jesus had talked to him
from the sky!

All Paul wanted to do was wait and pray. But then God sent a
man named Ananias to help Paul understand Jesus, to help him see,
to help him be baptized, and to help him begin his new life. Paul
became one of the strongest believers of all time in God and Jesus.

From that day on, Paul told everyone he could about Jesus and
Jesus' love. He told people that he met on the streets. He traveled
across the seas to teach people about Jesus. He also wrote letters
to Christians in faraway lands to help them understand Jesus' love.

Let's look at some of Paul's letters in the Bible.

(Flip through the pages of the New Testament. Once you come to Paul's first letter of Romans, continue the script and continue to proceed through Paul's other letters)

Here we find Paul's letter about Jesus to the Christians in Rome. Next he wrote two letters to the churches in Corinth. He also wrote letters to people in Galatia, Ephesus, Philippi, and Colossae. He wrote two letters to the people of Thessalonica. And last, he wrote letters about Jesus to his friends: Timothy, Titus, and Philemon. In these letters, Paul spoke about being thankful to God, about Jesus' Last Supper, about Jesus' love, and many other things.

Can we take some time today to write letters, just like Paul? I think we could write one to *(insert the name of someone else in your home or nearby: parent, grandparent, sibling, or neighbor)*. Are you ready? Here is our paper and pencil. Just like Paul, we should say who this letter is being written for. So "Dear *(insert the name)*,"

(Depending on your child's age and writing ability, let them write a few of the words or even just a few of the letters of the alphabet. Continue writing from the script)

"Today I learned about Paul's letters. I want to write a letter about Jesus too. Do you know how much Jesus loves you? Well, he does. I love you too. I am thankful that I know you and that we are a family in Jesus Christ. Love, *(insert child's name)*.

I don't know if Paul decorated his letters, but we can decorate ours with these markers if you want. Now, let's put it in the envelope and in the mailbox.

Do you want to write another one?

(Continue more letters as time and your child's attention span allow)

Look at us! Just like Paul with his letters, we are making a difference in the world with our letters. We are telling people about Jesus' love. I am proud of us, and I bet God is too.

Seasonal Christmas Lessons

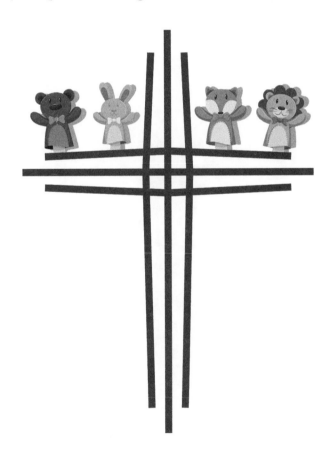

Week 44: The Lord's Signs

BIBLE READING: Isaiah 7:14

Dear Parent,

Now it's time to begin preparing your children's hearts for the celebration of Christmas and the birth of Jesus. To achieve this, open your children's eyes to the signs all around us. Man-made signs at every street corner have several purposes. They can add to our knowledge, require our obedience, or facilitate our safety. Come to think of it, God also gives us signs for the same reasons: knowledge, obedience, and safety. Regardless whether made by man or by God, signs give us guidance. Thanks be to God for those that point to Jesus!

Materials:

Bible, access to the outdoors and, if necessary, a mode of transportation

Script:

Have you ever seen a sign?

(Let your child answer)

Let's go outside and see if we can find a sign.

(There should be signs outside, even if you are in a residential area; however, if you need to drive in a car or take a walk to see a sign, now is the time to do so. Discuss the signs you see with your child. This lesson refers to three types of signs; keep in mind every sign should fall into one of these categories: safety, knowledge, or obedience)

Here is a street-name sign. This sign gives us knowledge. It tells us the name of this street and helps us to know where we are. It's important to know where we are. When we know where we are, we can find where we are going. We should be thankful for this sign, because of the knowledge it gives us.

Here is a no-parking sign. This sign doesn't make us more knowledgeable. Do you know what this sign is for? This sign is here for obedience and to help us follow the rules. We can't park right there. The town *(insert: shopkeeper, residents)* and the police don't want us to park there. We should be thankful for this sign because it helps us to obey and make good choices.

Here is a stop sign. Why do you think it is here?

(Let your child answer)

Does it help with traffic? Does it keep a car right here safe from the cars driving over there? Because of this stop sign there will not be a car crash, and people will not get hurt. We should be thankful for this sign because it keeps people safe.

(After you finish discussing the signs you and your child found together, walk together to see more signs. Continue with script while walking)

These signs were all made by people. But there are more signs in this world too. God gives us signs. God's signs can also give us knowledge, require obedience, and keep us safe.

It would be interesting if God used bright red, white, yellow, and green signs to tell us stuff. But sometimes, he doesn't use bright colors or even words. Sometimes, God's signs are a little harder to see or hear. It is important that we think about God every day so that he can reach us when he wants to give us a sign.

Back in the time before Jesus was born, God gave the people many signs to tell them that Jesus was coming. The Bible says, "The Lord will give you a sign: the virgin will conceive and give birth to a son, and will call him Immanuel" (Isaiah 7:14). Immanuel means "God with us," and it refers to Jesus. The three wise men, who wanted to come visit baby Jesus didn't know where Jesus was going to be born. They didn't have a big yellow street sign with an arrow to show them where to go. But do you know what "sign" from God *was* there to give them knowledge of where they were and show them where to go?

(Let your child answer)

The Christmas star was a sign leading them all the way to baby Jesus in the manger!

Joseph was given a sign from God too. He didn't get instructions from a bright-colored sign to know he should still marry Mary, even though the child she was carrying was not his. Joseph had a dream that told him what to do. This sign from God required his obedience. And Joseph did obey.

After the wise men met baby Jesus, they received another sign, which kept them safe. It wasn't a big, red stop sign, but rather a dream. The dream was a sign from God telling them which route would get them home safely and which route wouldn't.

God gives us signs. We just have to keep our eyes open to see them. We have to be quiet and listen to hear them. We have to meet up with God in prayer every day . . . just in case he wants to give us a sign.

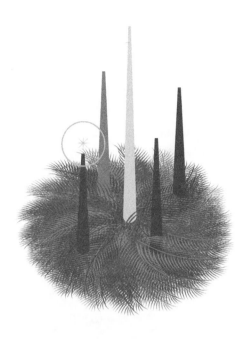

Week 45:
Advent Wreath and Faith

BIBLE READING: Isaiah 7:14 and excerpts from the

book of Matthew

Dear Parent,

For the next four weeks, you'll continue to prepare your children's hearts for the celebration of Jesus' birth at Christmas. Every year, we work hard around the house to get ready for the holiday season. And, being ever mindful of the "reason for the season," you may want to add Bible playtime to your traditions of baking cookies and singing Christmas carols. You might be thinking, "Add another to-do item to Christmastime?!" But this addition is one that will hopefully allow you to stop, reflect, and quietly prepare your own heart and your children's hearts for the peace and love of Jesus Christ during Christmas.

Materials:

Bible, five candles (traditionally three purple, one pink, and one white—but any color works), one wreath, real or fake greenery and floral pieces, small Christmas ornaments, and small lettering to spell out five words on your wreath: faith, peace, hope, love, and joy

NOTE: Whatever materials you have on hand will be fine. The activity is what is important, not the color and size of your supplies. Although the materials list is longer this week, these will be used over the course of the next four weeks. This image shows how the wreath generally comes together.

Script:

I love this time of year! December is one of my favorite months! We must get ready for Jesus' birthday, which, you know, is the reason we celebrate Christmas! There is so much to do around the house to get ready. But, more importantly, there is much to do in our hearts to get ready.

I want to begin making an Advent wreath today. Will you make it with me?

(Let your child answer)

Let's think about the word Advent. Advent means "coming," and Jesus' birthday is coming. Now, let's think about this wreath. What shape is a wreath?

(Let your child answer)

Yes, it is in the shape of a circle. Circles are never ending. Jesus' love is never ending.

(Trace the outline of the wreath's circle with your finger. Show how there is no end)

So, we will turn this simple wreath into an Advent wreath! It won't hang on a door anymore; rather it will sit on our table to teach us more about Jesus as Christmas approaches. By the time of Jesus' birthday, we will have decorated our Advent wreath with five candles. We will light one candle each week for the four weeks that we prepare for Jesus, and we will still have one left over to light on Christmas Eve.

Just like we are building the Advent wreath in stages, we will decorate the wreath in stages. Before we know it, the wreath will grow into a lovely Christmas decoration that we can reuse every year. The best part is that by the time the wreath is ready for Christmas, our hearts will be ready for Christmas too!

Now, let's put the first candle through the boughs of the wreath.

(If it will fit through the ring of the actual wreath, great. If not, put the candle inside the circle of the wreath and add greenery to make the candle look attached)

Perfect! Let's add some more greenery around the first candle and in the middle. This candle represents *faith*. If we don't have faith, our hearts won't be ready for Christmas!

What is *faith*? Faith means believing in something without questioning it, and, sometimes, it means believing in something you can't see. Let's look at the Bible together and see what it tells us about faith . . .

> *(Turn to the book of Matthew. Find the first page and the last page, so that you are holding the whole section of the book of Matthew in your hand)*

All of these words are written for us to learn things about Jesus. A lot of these words have to do with faith in Jesus and God.

In this one part of the Bible between my fingers, Jesus talks about how important faith is fourteen times! Jesus wants us to have faith in him. He wants us to believe in him without questioning. He wants us to believe in him even when we can't see him.

In the Bible, when people have faith and believe in Jesus, their fears don't scare them, their storms don't break them, and their sicknesses don't hurt them. In the Bible, when people have faith and believe in Jesus, their broken legs can walk, their blind eyes can see, and their hunger is fed. In the Bible, when people have faith and believe in Jesus, the winds that blow hard can be calmed down, the mountains can be moved, and the thoughts that hurt can be gone forever. All of these things actually happen because of faith.

Our faith in Jesus makes anything possible. And our faith in Jesus can make our hearts happier as we go through each and every day. So I know I have faith in Jesus.

Do you believe and have faith in Jesus, without question and without even seeing him?

> *(Let your child answer)*

Well, that is great! Now we can decorate the Faith portion of our Advent wreath. I have some lettering here, so we can spell out faith and put it by our faith candle. Let's add some little decorations to our Advent wreath too.

> *(Enjoy the decorating together)*

Week 46:
Advent Wreath and Peace

BIBLE READING: Luke 1:30–33 and John 14:27

Dear Parent,

   This week, you'll focus on the theme of Peace
as you continue building and enjoying your Advent
wreath. In this busy and hectic time of year, it will
be a blessing to stop, find some quiet time with your
child, and reflect on the peace that only Jesus can
give us. May you enjoy this preparation of all of your
family's hearts for the celebration of Jesus' birth and
the peace that comes with it!

Materials:

   Bible, last week's Advent wreath, the second candle, more
decorations: greenery and floral pieces, small Christmas ornaments

(bulbs, crosses, stars, or fruit), lettering for the word "Peace," flashlight, and a blanket

Script:

I had so much fun last week when we started decorating our Advent wreath. I can't believe it is already time to sit down and make the next part. Christmastime goes by so fast. In our second week of getting ready for Jesus' birthday, our house decorations and plans are coming along for the big Christmas celebration, but we still have a lot to do to get our hearts ready to celebrate.

I have a question about last week. Can you remember the name we gave the first candle?

(Let your child answer)

Yes, the answer is Faith, which we now know means believing in Jesus without questioning or even seeing him.

Now, let's put the second candle through the boughs of the wreath. Perfect! Let's put some of the extra greenery around the second candle, and let's fill some more into the middle of the wreath too. It will be so lovely when it is finished!

Let's talk about this second candle. This candle represents *peace*. If we don't have peace, our hearts won't be ready for Christmas! What is peace? Do you know?

(Let your child answer)

Peace means calm and quiet goodness in your heart and in your mind.

(Speak slowly)

When we have faith in Jesus and believe in him, something wonderful happens to us. We don't have to have worry and fear anymore. Those bad things are gone. The thing that is left is peace: the calm and quiet goodness in your heart and in your mind.

So when there is a thunderstorm outside and you begin to feel scared, all you have to do is take a deep breath, remember Jesus is with you, and let all the worries and fears go away. Jesus wants you to have peace: the calm and quiet goodness in your heart and in your mind.

When are some other times that we might need to give our worries and fears to Jesus, and let him give us peace?

(Let your child answer. If necessary help your child remember times when peace is needed—a hard day at school or work, a bad dream . . .)

Peace is a gift from Jesus. Let's see what the Bible says about Peace.

(Turn to John 14:27)

These are words about peace that Jesus said, "Peace I leave with you; my peace I give you. I do not give to you as the world gives. Do not let not your hearts be troubled and do not be afraid" (John 14:27).

Let's sit here silently and see if we can practice feeling peace. Close your eyes. Think of Jesus hugging you.

(Pause. While your child's eyes are closed, give them a hug)

Keep your eyes closed. Think of the light in heaven shining on you.

(Pause. Shine a bright flashlight down onto your child)

Think of the warmth of God's love all around you.

(Pause. Wrap a soft blanket around your child)

Do you feel peace? Do you feel the calm and quiet goodness in your heart and in your mind?

Now, keep your eyes closed, and imagine walking down the street while Jesus is hugging you, the light is shining on you, and the warmth is moving with you. It feels peaceful, doesn't it?

Can you imagine being at school with all of those things surrounding you?

(Pause)

Can you imagine your next play date with all of those things surrounding you?

(Pause)

Open your eyes. There are a bunch of things in this world that I could be afraid of or worried about. But Jesus gives me peace. I can have calm and quiet goodness in my heart and in my mind whenever I want.

Last week, we realized we do have faith, and this week we realize we truly have peace! Let's decorate the Peace section of our Advent wreath. I have some lettering to help us spell out peace. Let's put it by our peace candle. We can use these little decorations too.

(Enjoy the decorating together)

Week 47:
Advent Wreath and Hope

BIBLE READING: Luke 1:35–38 and Romans 15:4

Dear Parent,

This week, you'll focus on the theme of Hope as you continue building and enjoying your Advent wreath. The lesson is not just for your child; may your own heart be filled with hope, anticipating the celebration of Jesus' "coming."

Materials:

Bible, the Advent wreath, the third candle, greenery and floral pieces, small Christmas ornaments, lettering for the word "Hope," and an ice pack

Script:

Let's sit down and make the next part of our Advent wreath! It is our third week of getting ready for Jesus' birthday, and our hearts are getting more and more ready to celebrate. Can you remember the name we gave the first candle?

(Let your child answer)

Yes, the answer is Faith, which we now know means believing in Jesus.

Can you remember the name we gave the second candle?

(Let your child answer)

Yes, the answer is Peace, which is that calm and quiet goodness in our hearts and in our minds that comes from believing in Jesus.

It is time to put the third candle through the boughs of the wreath. Let's put some of the extra greenery around the third candle, and fill the middle of the wreath in more too. It will be so lovely when it is finished! We have just one more week after this one!

Now, let's talk about this third candle. This candle represents *hope*. Do you know what hope is?

(Let your child answer)

Hope is a good feeling about what might happen.

Have you ever hoped for anything?

(Let your child answer)

I have hoped for many things. Last time you were sick, I hoped you would get well. Last time we had a picnic, I hoped it would last longer. Last time we were in a big traffic jam, I hoped we would get home safely.

Hope doesn't just happen. It is a process that comes from knowing Jesus. Let's look at the process in the steps that our Advent wreath has taught us. We have *faith* in Jesus and believe in him. He gives us *peace*, which makes us feel better. By feeling better, we have *hope* that more good things will happen.

Faith, peace, and hope are important and necessary in our lives.

Let's think about them with an example, like a playtime injury. Let's pretend we were playing today, and we fell.

> *(Lay on the ground with your child, both of you holding your elbows as if you bumped them. Put the ice pack on your child and continue with the script)*

Ouch! If we didn't have faith in Jesus, we wouldn't find peace through the pain. Then, we wouldn't have hope that we would heal quickly. We would only think about the part of your body that hurts. It would be hard to get through that injury without Jesus.

> *(Stand up together)*

Let's act out the whole thing again, but this time let's do it with Jesus in our lives.

> *(Lay on the ground with your child, both of you holding your elbows as if you bumped them. Put the ice pack on your child and continue with the script)*

Ouch! This time we do have faith in Jesus. We are definitely hurting, but we feel peace that we are not alone. Then, we have hope for quick healing. We feel blessed that our legs and head aren't hurt. We know we will get through this injury with Jesus' help.

Everything is better with Jesus in our lives. Otherwise, the hard stuff would just seem too hard. So do we have hope? Yes, we do! Well this is great!

I have some lettering so we can spell out hope and put it by our Hope candle.

Now that we have spelled out hope, I would like to read a verse from the Bible about hope.

In Romans 15:4, it says, "For everything that was written in the past was written to teach us, so that through the endurance taught in the Scriptures and the encouragement they provide we might have hope."

Should we decorate around our Hope candle then too? I have some little decorations here.

> *(Enjoy more decorating)*

Week 48:
Advent Wreath and Love

BIBLE READING: John 3:16

Dear Parent,

This week, you'll discuss God's love as you add the Love candle to your Advent wreath. Enjoy this special time with your child!

Materials:

Bible, your Advent wreath, the fourth candle, greenery and floral pieces, small Christmas ornaments, two small human-like figurines, and the lettering for "Love"

Script:

It's time to sit down and make the next part of our Advent wreath! This is our fourth week of getting ready for Jesus' birthday, and our hearts are getting more and more ready to celebrate.

Can you remember the name we gave the first candle?

(Let your child answer)

Yes, the answer is Faith.
Can you remember the name we gave the second candle?

(Let your child answer)

The answer is Peace.
I have one more question for you. Can you remember the name we gave our third candle?

(Let your child answer)

The answer is Hope, and hope is having good feelings about what might happen because we know Jesus.

Now let's put the fourth candle through the boughs of the wreath. Let's put some of the extra greenery around the fourth candle, and fill some more into the middle of the wreath too.

Can we talk about this fourth candle? This candle represents *love*. Well, we know all about love, don't we?

We do know about love because we give it to each other every day. I am your parent, and I love you. You are my child, and you love me. Can you guess who loves all of us? Yes, God does! God is the father of everything good in the whole world. God is our parent, and he loves us. We are his children, and we love him.

Let's see what the Bible says about Love. John 3:16 says, "For God so loved the world that he gave his one and only Son." God does love us. But it's kind of hard to think about sometimes because he is so huge. I mean, he is God. He is as big as the heavens and bigger than the earth.

Now look at you and me. We are just two small human beings out of seven billion on the earth. Look at how big you are and how tiny this little figurine is. Imagine you are God and you're trying to hug this little guy. It's hard to hug, isn't it? And, it would be hard to show it your love too, right?

Our huge God wanted to find a way to reach our little selves, to be on our level, to help us look into the eyes of his love, and to learn to live how he wants us to live. So what did God do? God sent Jesus. He made Jesus a human. Jesus could be our size. He could talk to us and teach us lessons. Jesus could love us here on earth and show us how God loves us from the heavens.

Look at this second figurine right next to the first one. Pretend it is Jesus right next to you.

When I see them together, I can understand that they are now on the same level, can reach each other, hug each other, teach each other, live like each other, share feelings with each other, and give love to each other. It makes sense that God sent us Jesus, doesn't it?

If we think about the season of Advent, what day was the very first day that Jesus was on earth to begin showing us God's love?

(Let your child answer)

Christmas day is the first day Jesus was here! God gives us his love through Jesus, and that love is why we celebrate Christmas. So let's decorate the Love section of our Advent wreath. I have some lettering so we can spell out love and put it by our Love candle. I have some little decorations here too.

(Enjoy more decorating)

Week 49:
Christmas Eve and
the Advent Wreath's Joy

BIBLE READING: Luke 2:4–7 and Luke 2:8–14

Dear Parent,

You are almost there! Tomorrow is Christmas, and you probably have many tasks to finish and plans to fulfill beforehand. Today's message is brief yet simple: Merry Christmas! May your Christmas with your precious children be enveloped in joy. You and your children are ready to celebrate the joyful day Jesus Christ was born.

Materials:

Bible, your Advent wreath, the fifth candle, lettering for "Joy"

Script:

Our Advent wreath is almost finished! Before Christmas Day comes tomorrow, we have one more candle to add. But first, let's think about what we have learned so far this Advent season while we've been getting our hearts ready for Christmas.

The first candle is _____(Faith).

The second candle is _____(Peace).

The third candle is _____(Hope).

The fourth candle is _____(Love).

Yes! And now, our fifth and final candle represents *Joy*! Of course, it is joy! Joy makes perfect sense! How do we feel when we think about Jesus Christ being born? We feel joy! How do we feel when we know we have faith, when we have peace, when we have hope, and when we have Jesus' love poured into us? We then feel joy!

So what is the name of the last candle to complete our wreath and to make us totally ready for Jesus' birthday? It is Joy! Well, then, let's put the Joy candle in the center of the wreath.

The Bible says in Luke 2:8–14:

> And there were shepherds living out in the fields nearby, keeping watch over their flocks at night. An angel of the Lord appeared to them, and the glory of the Lord shone around them. . . . The angel said to them, "Do not be afraid. I bring you good news that will cause great joy for all the people. Today in the town of David a Savior has been born to you; he is the Messiah, the Lord. . . . Suddenly a great company of the heavenly host appeared with the angel, praising God and saying, "Glory to God in the highest heaven, and on earth peace to those on whom his favor rests!" (Luke 2:8–14)

Merry Christmas, my child. Because of Jesus, we have joy. We can get to know God through Jesus. One day, far from now, we will end up in a heavenly place with our awesome God because Jesus Christ was born, because Jesus lived, and because he saved us. I just didn't want to celebrate Christmas without telling you that.

Now let's put the joy lettering onto our Advent wreath and finish anything else we need to before tomorrow's amazing day!

Week 50: Christmas Gifts

BIBLE READING: Matthew 2:9–11

Dear Parent,

 The goal of this week's lesson is to teach your children why we give gifts at Christmas. There are many folk tales and theories as to where this tradition started. But chronologically, the first gift given on the first Christmas Day was the gift of life to us through Jesus Christ (John 3:16). Another explanation from the Bible pertains to the wise men, also called the three kings. They were called to leave their lands for an arduous journey to find the "King of the Jews" (Matthew 2:2), and they showed their loving adoration with gifts of gold, frankincense, and myrrh.

Materials:

Bible, three gift bags with a piece of candy in each, two robes or capes or blankets, two crowns or headbands, a baby doll or stuffed animal, a snack (at least twenty-four raisins or small crackers or grapes), and two small bags to carry materials

Script:

(Plan to take a nice walk, like the three wise men did, even if it's just making laps inside your home. Before you begin, lay the baby doll in the place you'll finish your walk, to represent baby Jesus)

Well, wasn't Christmas morning wonderful? What was your favorite part?

(Let your child answer)

My favorite part was thinking about how Jesus was born on that day over two thousand years ago and how lucky I am to have him in my life.

What was your second favorite part of Christmas morning?

(Let your child answer)

My second favorite part of Christmas morning was giving you a gift. Do you know why we give gifts on Christmas morning?

(Let your child answer)

We give gifts to each other because God gave Jesus to us. The biggest gift in the whole wide world is the gift of life through Jesus Christ. Another reason we give gifts at Christmas is because there were gifts given during that first Christmas. Did you know that? The Bible says that three wise men brought gifts to Jesus.

The wise men were kings in their faraway lands. Can you imagine being one of those kings? You are all warm and cozy in your awesome palace, and all of a sudden you feel like you should get up. All of a sudden, you know you must leave on a long journey. All of a sudden, you realize you must find baby Jesus, the King of kings.

So they put on their robes. Let's put on our robes. They packed their crowns. Let's pack our crowns. They brought some food to eat on the long journey. Let's bring our food. Last, they gathered gifts for baby Jesus! Let's gather ours. I have three bags here, but let's not look inside them until we find our pretend baby Jesus.

Now, let's leave our palaces in search of this new king who has just been born! How do we know where to go? Do you know how they found baby Jesus? They followed a star; let's pretend to follow one too.

(Take a nice long walk, following the script as you go)

It is said that twelve days passed between the day Jesus was born and the day the wise men found him. Other sources say it was two years. How about for the sake of today's lesson we use the twelve-day theory? Has it been one pretend day yet? Can we stop for dinner?

(Stop walking and have a bite of snack up to twelve separate times. Show your child how passionately the wise men were in their calling to find the child in the manger, without taking so long you lose their attention. Continue with the "Are we there yet?" and "Let's keep going on this long and hard journey" mentality for up to twelve walks and twelve "dinners." Finish the "twelfth day" of the journey at the baby doll representing Jesus)

Whew! We have been going and going. Now, it is the twelfth day! And there is baby Jesus! This day is called *Epiphany.* Epiphany is a very special day in churches around the world. It marks the end of the wise men's journey, celebrates their finding of Jesus, and is always on January sixth, which is twelve days after Christmas.

That first Christmas season, the wise men were so happy and excited to be near Jesus. They showed their thankfulness for his birth. And also, they gave him their gifts. My child, that is why we give gifts at Christmas. We are like the wise men. We are so happy and excited to be nearer to Jesus. Like the wise men, we want to show our thankfulness for his birth. We want to give gifts at Christmas too.

Now let's see what's in these little bags for our pretend baby Jesus here!

(Enjoy the treats and the rest of your Christmas holiday)

Final Thoughts and Lessons

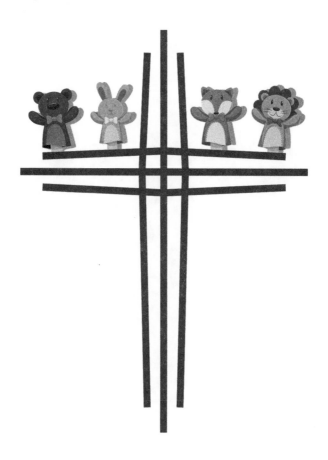

Week 51:
From Bead to Necklace;
From Christian to Church

BIBLE READING: Acts 2:42–47

Dear Parent,

 The goal of this week's lesson is to help your children understand the importance of being part of a church community. We'll use a bead as a metaphor. When it stands alone, a bead is beautiful and sturdy. However, many beads strung together can become a strong necklace, and many Christians strung together can become a strong church. Praise God for our churches and our communities of faith.

Materials:

 Bible, two pieces of string measuring two feet, and enough beads to fit onto and fill up the strings

Script:

I am so proud of how you have grown this year. We have been working on this book for many months, and you have learned so much about Jesus. You are like this lovely bead here.

(Take a bead in your hand)

You are well-rounded . . . like this bead.
You shine in the light around you . . . like this bead.
You are beautiful when you stand alone . . . like this bead.
Your faith is solid and sturdy . . . like this bead.

Do you know another characteristic of a bead? When a bead is next to more beads, it becomes bigger and stronger. It grows into something else. It becomes a necklace.

So, if you are this bead,

(Put your child's bead on the string)

And I am this bead,

(Put another bead on the string next to the bead representing your child)

And, *(insert the name of a Christian family member or Christian friend)* is this bead,

(Put another bead on the string next to the first two)

And, *(insert more names)* is this bead,

(Thread another bead next to the first three, and continue to do so for as many beads as you have to fill up the necklace)

When you put all of us "beads" together, we grow into a necklace, which is something that is even bigger and stronger than any one of us alone. This necklace made of beads reminds me of our church, which is made up of our church family members.

When you put all of us Christians together, we grow into a church, which is something that is even bigger and stronger than any one of us alone. And church is good. It makes God happy to see us worshipping and working alongside each other.

In the Bible, it says,

> They devoted themselves to the apostles' teaching
> and to the fellowship, to the breaking of bread and
> to prayer. Everyone was filled with awe at the many
> wonders and signs performed by the apostles. All
> the believers were together and had everything in
> common. . . . Every day they continued to meet
> together in the temple courts. They broke bread in
> their homes and ate together with glad and sincere
> hearts, praising God and enjoying the favor of all the
> people. And the Lord added to their number daily
> those who were being saved. (Acts 2:42–47)

This passage in the Bible describes the first church ever. It is also describing our church today.

Now, let's add more beads to our strings and make beautiful necklaces to help us remember how beautiful our church is and how, together, we become bigger and stronger than when we stand alone.

Week 52:
Where We Go from Here

BIBLE READING: 2 Corinthians 13:14

Dear Parent,

The goal of this week's lesson is to show your children where we go from here. Whether you plan to start a new devotional, join a new church, begin a new Bible study, or re-read this book, Jesus will be with you and your children wherever you go. As Paul said to the Corinthians in his second letter, and as one of my favorite pastors said to our congregation every Sunday, "May the grace of the Lord Jesus Christ and the love of God, and the fellowship of the Holy Spirit be with you all." (2 Corinthians 13:14)

Materials:

Bible, transportation-related toys in your home, such as a toy boat, train, car, bike, or plane)

Script:

Wow. I can't believe you and I have finished this book together—all fifty-two weeks! So now, where do we go from here? There are so many ways to continue to grow in our relationship with God through Jesus. I can't wait to get started on another spiritual journey with you. For our final lesson in this book, I want to talk about going places.

Back during Jesus' time, people traveled by camel and donkey. But now we have many more ways to go places. Can you think of how we can get from one place to another?

(Let your child answer)

Sure! We can walk, run, and bike. We can ride in cars, boats, trains, or even airplanes! If we sat and thought about it, I imagine we could think of a hundred different ways to go places.

Let's play with these ways to travel while we think about more ways to travel.

(Play together and continue with the script)

We could crawl, skip, or even hop. We could jump, ride horses, or skateboard.

(While you play together, continue to list ways to move and travel as long as your children would like to and as long as their attention span allows)

Do you want to know the one thing all these ways to travel have in common? No matter where we go or how we get there, Jesus will be with us all along the way.

(Enjoy your Bible playtime. And thanks for letting this author come along for the "ride." Godspeed!)

Connect with the Author

Website: www.playonword.com

Email: info@playonword.com

Follow our Facebook page:
Play on Word by Devin Lonergan Holt

Follow us on Instagram: @playonword